# Dark Psychology Secrets:

*Become Highly Effective to Analyze People*

*Find Out if Their Intention is Brainwashing by Discovering the 7 Habits of Dark Psychology*

# Table of Contents

# Chapter 1: Introduction

Psychology plays an important role in everyday life, including how we process information, become influenced, or influence others and how we make decisions. It is a study that focuses on the mind and behavior, with many sub-groups or fields of research. In this book, the focus is on dark psychology. Dark psychology is a study of a specific human condition that involves predator and prey behavior, the ability of humans to manipulate and victimize another living being, and how likely certain types of people are more susceptible to acting on these impulses than others. The study of dark psychology is an interesting and revealing field that uncovers how common it is for people to use tools of mind control and manipulation for their own gain, even at the risk of harming someone else.

Dark psychology can be divided into three sub-categories, known collectively as the dark triad:

- Narcissism

- Machiavellianism

- Psychopathy

Narcissism is defined as a personality disorder where a person becomes obsessed or fixated on a perfect, idealized version of who they are. They are self-centered and arrogant, manipulate and unable to accept any criticism, even if it is constructive. A narcissist is prone to fantasizing about having lots of power, beauty, wealth, popularity and anything else that places them in a position of importance and worship.

Machiavellianism is a trait personality that describes a person with a keen focus on themselves, above everyone else. They will seek to manipulate, exploit, and betray other people for their gain, with little or no regard for anyone else. They tend to be cold and ruthless in their methods and fixated on power, even more than narcissists. Since a person with this personality trait is cynical of other people, not trusting anyone, they are eager to manipulate and control whomever they can to reach the top.

Psychopathy is an anti-social disorder that is characterized by a lack of empathy, remorse, or connection with other people. A person with this personality will manipulate, use and work around other people and situations to get what they want.

They don't have the capacity to feel what others' do, nor do they have the ability to form a bond like most people.

The three above personality disorders combine to form the dark triad, which is a malignant and dangerous mix that can negatively impact and seriously damage a person's life. When we imagine the types of people who fit into this category, or any one of the three toxic personalities, we might picture a convicted criminal or serial killer, though many people with these attributes could be someone we work with or know on a personal level. We may not realize a person has the traits of the dark triad until their techniques of manipulation and exploitation begin to have an impact on our lives.

### 1. How Does Psychology Play a Role in the World We Live In?

Psychology plays an important role in the world we live in, from how we interact with each other, make decisions, and shape our habits. It influences how we buy and use products and how we respond emotionally to people and situations. The major impact psychology has an effect on every aspect of life, whether we realize it or experience its impact subconsciously. While there are many positive results when psychology is applied in our decision making, in how understanding this study, even the basic science of it, can help us understand and connect with other people and resolve matters with the knowledge of why and how people think and behave. On the other hand, dark psychology focuses on the methods used to manipulate and coerce other people, often in a covert manner. There are different methods used to control and manipulate people, which will be covered in-depth in this book.

## 2.  How Media and People in our Life Impact Us

One of the most dramatic ways in which psychology shapes our actions is through media and our social network, whether it's online, in person, or both. The growing prevalence of internet use is now the mainstream in how we communicate, play, and work. Regular business, signing contracts and making major purchases and decisions are often accomplished online, sometimes with little or no thought. This can cause some regret later, or a lack of understanding of the responsibility and impact that decisions we make online has, from posting controversial comments and pictures to ruining relationships and friendships over misunderstandings and miscommunication. There are many reasons why social media has become detrimental in many people's lives:

- They are completely saturated in it, posting every moment of their lives, and leaving little offline, which is habit-forming, and may cause people to feel inadequate to others with better pictures or posts, and getting too fixated on what other people do online, instead of focusing on their own lives. It takes time away from family, friends, meals and other meaningful moments in life that don't need to be documented with social media posts

- We literally lose sleep over social media and similar platforms, because the content is consuming and involving. It can have the effect of staying in our minds and impact the way we look at ourselves and others. Aside from using technology too close to bedtime, which interferes with a good night's sleep. We often forget to adhere to a regular sleeping routine, which has a ripple effect the next morning.

- There have been positive improvements in the acceptance of more body sizes and types; however, many people struggle still when they become involved with the "perfect" images online, whether they are conventional models or people who have reached celebrity or popular status because of a unique look or style. When this occurs, it skews our view of what is real versus what we perceive as real. This has an impact on self-esteem, and causes a lot of people, predominantly women, and girls, to strive for unrealistic beauty standards to achieve popular status in society

- The level of connection is overdone, and while people are always online, whether they realize it or not, it becomes the norm after a while, requiring people to constantly "report" what they are doing, and answer messages often. This can be stressful for people who want to take a break from the constant attachment to social media. There is a heightened level of anxiety where people become worried about what others may think of them, and there is a constant need to achieve more and showcase it in a public forum.

- For a growing number of people, social interaction is confined to their technology, allowing them to opt-out of meeting with their friends and acquaintances. While social meetings and meetups are arranged online and lead to many healthy relationships and friendships in real life, excessive use of online forums and media can keep some people from interacting beyond the computer. This can be helpful for people with social anxiety, giving them a platform to communicate in a comfortable way, while for others, it can hinder their real-life connections with family and friends, by distractions from social media notifications and other sources.

The above factors indicate how social media and the use of technology can impact everyday living, affecting personal privacy, relationships and how we interact with the world we live in. Imagine the impact dark psychology would have with the same power to influence how we think and behave in life, which can often have a devastating effect on us and the people we care about. The next section covers the prevalence of subliminal messages and how they impact our mind and behavior.

### 3. Absorbing Messages and Subliminal Content in our Environment and How it Affects Us

Subliminal messages and information refer to covert or hidden items transmitted in broadcasts, videos and presentations, often through the use of commercial, news media outlets and more recently, social media, blogs, and forms. While the hidden ideas conveyed may not seem obvious at first, they have an immediate effect on the audience. Early studies on subliminal content focused on small or brief exposure to such messages indicated an impact almost immediately by triggering the reader or listener to react in a way consistent with the hidden information. This is due to the mind's ability to pick up on these minor or unnoticed items from the conscious side. Our subconscious has the ability to absorb much more that we see. For this reason, advertisements and media experts will cultivate their message and choose wording, images, and music that reflect what they want you to feel and react, even if the statement appears simple and obvious.

In studies initially conducted on subliminal content, the results seemed harmless and minimal, due to the short-term effects. Granted, the ads or videos were brief, which were reflected similarly in their reflective reactions. Consider the impact of such messages played repeatedly over a period of hours, days, weeks, or months.

The long-term results yield much stronger effects of covert content in these messages, including the ability to influence political ideas, commercial purchases, our mood, and attitudes towards certain people, groups and organizations. A person or group of people can be affected in such a way that a strongly held ethical or political belief can come into question, not like before, with the potential to sway or convince them to alter their decisions, including how they vote. In this way, subliminal content has a great impact on the masses, with the potential to shift an entire community, region or country into one direction or another. In commercials, there are bold statements and overt claims made to convince the audience that one product or service is superior to others. While we might question the validity, and feel we are in control of our decision to choose this product or not, there may be symbols, scenery or actions in the background that target the emotional side of our brain, seeking gratification as shown in the video or ad. Examples of ads that may subliminally influence our decision-making from one product over another include the following scenarios:

1. 1.A family is on a beach, enjoying their vacation on a sunny day. They are all physically appealing in appearance and look content and relaxed. The ad may show a few scenes of activities, from water-skiing, and boating to sunbathing, which eventually creates an abundance of thirst. This can be easily satisfied with a can of soda nestled in a cooler of ice. As

one of the parents opens a chilled can, as their thirsty family members look on, their facial expression shows a delicate sign of relief because their need to hydrate is satisfied, and their thirst is quenched. As the commercial closes, all family members show a facial expression of deep satisfaction after just one sip of the soda.

How would this ad impact someone watching it for the first time? Some people may enjoy soda on a regular basis, while others may avoid this drink due to high sugar, calories, and additives. In watching this ad, the soda-drinker who regularly enjoys this beverage knows the drawbacks of high sugar, and may consider cutting back, may suddenly feel a sense of reassurance in watching the family consume it. They may not realize that this reaction is based on the "happy family", though it may result in continuing to purchase soda, even an increase in consumption, despite its ill effects on their health. The non-soda drinker might consider enjoying this beverage on occasion due to the positive scenery, perfect weather and beautiful family in combination with the drink. In a sense, they are buying more than the drink; they are buying the full package they see on the television screen: the sunny beach, the happy family and satisfaction.

2. During a political campaign, several candidates air their appeal to voters for support of their party. One ad opens with photographs or footage of a rival political candidate, indicating their errors during their current or previous position, or other misdeeds or scandals. These are embellished and broadcast in a matter-of-fact manner, and while the visuals accompanying the speech are quick, they are a stark contrast to the political party paying for the broadcast, inadvertently showing them as the "good guy". These types of ads may not indicate any solutions or platform highlights, which makes them appear like smear campaigns for the opposition. The way they are presented, however, tries to convince the audience that they are doing you a favor, by bringing certain items of concern to your attention, such as these examples:

"Do you want your tax money spent on their lavish vacations? Do you feel confident that your tax dollars will go to the services you need?"

"How can you trust a candidate to be a responsible politician after they were involved in (details of scandal)"

"You deserve the best person/party for the job."

Making these bold statements may not be subliminal, and often, people who are well-read and politically savvy may ignore these messages, labeling them as propaganda. For people who are undecided or "on the fence", these campaigns serve as a powerful tool for persuasion, especially with visuals and dramatic music in the background, serving as the subliminal content, which strengthens the overall purpose of the ad.

Over the course of time, where subliminal content is continuously broadcast to the public, there is a greater chance of influencing behavior and action on a long-term basis. Studies on recurring messages indicate that where the mind is open to making free choices without restriction between several options, the presence of hidden or subliminal material can significantly persuade the choice in favor of the ad, unbeknownst to the would-be consumer, who becomes more likely to choose one product or service over another, even without the impact of pricing or other factors.

## 4. Fantasy vs. Reality in Media, Social Media and Within Our Immediate Community

Social media is a part of most people's daily lives. When we view our friends and coworkers' profiles online, we will often find perfect photographs and depictions of the perfect life: the happy family, ideal career, and vacation experiences. You may notice how each picture is without flaws and/or with filters, posted in between inspirational quotes and popular memes. Social media extends past the everyday casual life of family and friends. Numerous platforms are used by government organizations, corporations, and academic institutions. One person's image and background can be made available to millions online and on various websites and forums. You might use one platform for engaging in dialogue and discussions under the guise of a username to conceal the identity and use your real name and background information on a professional networking site for seeking employment and business opportunities. In all cases, what we portray online is a version of our real selves, though it is not a complete picture of who we really are. This results in a blurred version of who others imagine us to be versus our authentic selves.

How does social media skew who we really are and reinvent our identity online? One of the major reasons lies in how algorithms process billions of pieces of data and present this to the users of these sites, viewing profiles with stunning visuals and banners, not just in content, but also layout and color-coordination. Have you ever noticed how one platform will change the format of pictures and designs of the website, which can alter the appearance of certain accounts to appear bolder or more enhanced than before? This can have the effect of embellishing or extenuating certain features that were nearly invisible before, such as background photos, highlights from certain posts. There are also enhancements made available on certain websites to alter photographs and connect people in such a way that their relationships appear flawless and perfect, and their physical appearance much different than reality. As our lives become busier with work and commitments, we become increasingly more reliant on our online personas and those of people we know and see less often. Over the course of time, we view the online version as the "real" person, forgetting or dismissing anything that doesn't align with the virtual or "fantasy" profile.

Another way algorithms can impact what we see online is by streaming certain news events and messages more frequently than others, giving us a biased view or unbalanced access to one side or perspective. We may also see more posts from one or a few news sources more than others, which makes it seem as though we're only seeing part of the picture, and only from a specific political or social and economic stance. While this is a highly debatable issue, not only the skewing or favoritism of some sources and posts over others but the prevalence of certain groups or organizations that seem to have a strong following only because of their repetitious posts. In some cases, where organizations pay to showcase or advertise their messages and ads, there will be a dominant trail of posts and updates from these sources, even if their validity is questionable or seen as less legitimate.

Considering how common it is for most people to view social media information, profiles, and updates 24-7 at any time on a mobile device, computer or tablet, there is going to be a significant effect on how we view the world around us versus what our reality is. How can we make a clear and definitive distinction between the two worlds that coexist in our perception? Imagine meeting someone from a company or event online, noting their profile, pictures, and posts, only to find they look and act contrary to their social media account, even to the point of being deceitful? On the other hand, many people may exaggerate their accomplishments or experiences online, though they do so without any ill intentions or hidden agendas. We might think that someone is living a much happier and better life than us, only because they report or post when someone outstanding happens. Some people might post something noteworthy or exciting to compete with others, taking more pictures than usual and using filters or enhancements to make them appear brighter or more exciting. Even where a person is living a life of travel and adventure, it's important to note that they will go through many periods of boredom and normal struggles as most people do. Everything we read and view online is there because someone chose to post it. In real life, we see everything as it unfolds and occurs, whether it is exciting or uneventful because there are no filters or edits in real-time to alter what we experience in person versus how we portray and see the same events online.

Social media platforms allow many people from all parts of the world and backgrounds to connect, converse, and share in a world where barriers are removed, and unlikely friends and alliances are established. You may find yourself discussing classic rock music with someone on the other side of the world, or find someone who enjoys the same works of literature, cuisine, and films as you, even where there is a difference in culture and/or language.

# Chapter 2: Finding the Deception: Fantasy vs. Reality and the Dynamics of the World We See vs. the World We Live In

Recent articles and studies highlight the impact that our own sense of perception and the unrealistic version we see online can have on our mental health and well-being. When we see social media personas and news perceived as accurate and real, it may seem as though our own lives are meaningless or less impactful by comparison. This is because we are comparing every minute and part of our everyday existence to the selected posts and information posted online. We are making an unrealistic match between ourselves and other people because we only have a part of the equation. Likewise, another person could look at your profile and posts, even those you consider ordinary or uninteresting, and view them as better or more captivating than their own. In realizing these skewed realities and how our vision is shifted, we can see a pattern in what is real and imagined based on the limited and highlighted events of others on their profiles and social media accounts.

In all forms of media and projection on television, at work, or in public spaces, we can exhibit a different version of ourselves than we really are. For some people, which includes the majority, we might conceal our weaknesses, for example, or speak about our accomplishments and the people we find important in life. People who are manipulative or cunning will project a very different personality from who they really are, creating an image of someone who is charming, well-liked, and exciting, drawing people towards them and gaining their trust. We may not realize the impact this outward projection or false identity has on us until we learn the true nature of the person(s). As with any situation, it can be difficult to face a stark difference between reality and fantasy (or perceived reality), especially when all prior indicators support the false perception. This may cause confusion and wonder as to what is real and imagined, based on all the skewed facts, news reports and algorithms that push some items to the forefront of our minds, while others are ignored or avoided altogether.

5.  **Shifting Our Minds From the Fantasy Into Reality**

From a young age, most people are taught not to believe everything we hear and see, even though we may be taught or convinced to believe in concepts or ideologies that we later find to be false or questionable. This can shake anyone's idea of what is real or false, based on early childhood experiences and the resulting trauma, when we discover the truth. Throughout our lives, we will encounter situations that cause us to question what we believe or know to be true:

- Betrayal of a spouse or friend, which leads to a break-up or loss of friendship. At the very least, the relationship will never be regarded in the same manner following the incident(s), leading to a lack of trust.

- Learning of a hidden family secret later in life, and feeling misled as a result

- Transitioning from childhood into adulthood and learning about the reality of earning a living, a competitive workplace and other realities, some of the harder to adjust to than others. These may have been minimized or not explained in depth before, or seem much different than our own perception.

These experiences and many others will typically encourage you to question aspects of life itself, even from a philosophical viewpoint, about your personal beliefs, which can alter a person's life and mindset completely. Our relationships with other people are often not as they seem, and while many people are an "open book", without anything to hide or mask, other people may purposely or unintentionally conceal certain aspects of their personality to make a better impression of themselves. In looking at the world we live in, and all that we see and perceive, there are three main categories of what we encounter and experience:

- Illusions

- Fantasies

- Realities

Illusions are falsely held beliefs that we may hold onto because we sincerely feel they are accurate because of their similarities to the reality we know in our life. Illusions can be based on something that is real, which makes it easier to believe than fantasy, which is a complete fabrication of falsehood.

Fantasies are completely disconnected from reality and without any boundaries or limits. They can be anything and everything you can imagine, and reality doesn't apply in any way or form. Illusions, while they are similar to fantasy, they have some root in reality or stem from a real event or action, which makes them more believable than fantasy.

Reality is the actual existence of what you see, hear, and experience first-hand, without any skewed reports or illusionary ideas. Once you discover the reality of a situation, depending on the severity between what you believed previously and the actual accounts of an event, it can be a shock and a challenging realization to face.

The following examples illustrate how we can experience the perception of a relationship or situation that isn't what it appears to be. In these cases, as long as we continue to hold onto the perceived reality (the illusion or fantasy), we run the risk of severe disappointment at some point in the experience.

**Example 1: Dating a Married Person**

Ivan is married to Joan, but he is seeing Mary secretly. He is honest about his marital status, and both Ivan and Mary keep their ongoing affair a secret. While Mary is aware of Ivan's marriage to Joan and has always known about this from the beginning of the relationship, she begins to fantasize about a new life with Ivan away from the constraints of his marriage, and as a way for Mary to escape a dull life living in a small apartment and working a dead-end job. Ivan is an executive with the ability to travel worldwide and speak at various functions and events. Mary has accompanied him, albeit in secret, to some events, imagining herself as his wife instead of Joan, who has a career of her own and cannot attend any events with her husband. Mary often fantasizes about being whisked away from her boring life into a castle or secluded island with Ivan, who treats her like royalty, giving her undivided attention and treating her to lavish dinners and events. While Mary continues to fantasize about this idealization of Ivan, in reality, Ivan has no interest in Mary, aside from occasional sex and companionship. At the beginning of their affair, Ivan made the boundaries clear, though Mary's imagination and the overwhelming need for a change in her life occupied her dreams of grandeur, which drew to an abrupt end when Ivan decided to stop seeing her completely. Had Ivan made any false promises to leave his wife for Mary, there may have been some merit to Mary believing they would be a couple someday, even if not on a tropical island or castle.

In order for Mary to move away from the delusion of her non-existent relationship with Ivan after he breaks it off, she must take a look at the reality of the situation and understand that her entire fantasy was based on a longing for more than what she had. Once she understands the reality of her situation, only then can she make a realistic plan to make the necessary changes to improve the quality of her career and life.

**Example 2: A Lesson in Deceit**

Leonard dates Hannah for a few months, and their relationship is better than any he's ever experienced before. Hannah is not only physically attractive, but she is also enthusiastic, witty and fun to be with. Leonard feels as though he's found the perfect soulmate, and without any foreseeable problems. As he gets to know Hannah better over the course of a year, there are some interesting developments that he notices, though chooses to avoid dealing with:

- Leonard has not yet met Hannah's parents, despite several promises that she will introduce them to him at some point. When he approaches her on this topic, she kindly avoids it, pretending like it's not a big deal, and to keep the relationship amicable and non-confronting, Leonard simply accepts the excuses she gives and drops the subject.

- Hannah has a difficult time finding gainful employment, despite claiming to have a degree in finance and years of experience in banking. Leonard questions this internally, and while he wants to ask her, he knows (and has found) this to be a sensitive topic, and he decides to not bring it up after a few failed attempts.

- There seem to be a few inconsistencies in what Hannah states versus how she lives and behaves. In reality, she suffers from Borderline Personality Disorder, which has complicated her life to the point where she is no longer on

speaking terms with her parents, has had a
string of failed relationships and employment
options. While she is skilled in math and
accounting, she didn't complete her degree and
had been struggling ever since, taking short-
term and unfulfilling jobs.

Leonard knows some of the struggles Hannah has faced and continues to deal with, though he has an illusion that she is capable of great accomplishments despite her challenges. Hannah has successfully convinced him that she is a prodigy that simply needs to be discovered to achieve greatness, and while the reality of her situation is far from this story, Leonard holds onto this belief, so that he may continue the relationship, despite the backlash of his own family and friends. They notice that he is being held "captive" by Hannah, and feel the frustration of not being able to do anything about it.

Until Leonard is in a position to take a realistic view of the situation, the facts, and determining that all that he holds sacred about Hannah is an illusion, hinging on fantasy, he will continue to live in denial of a relationship that is not sustainable. At some point, Hannah will experience increased erratic mood swings and behavior, including disappearing for days at a time, worrying Leonard, eventually causing him to question the validity of everything. He wants to delay facing the inevitable, because despite her deceiving him, Leonard loves Hannah, though he also realizes that their union will not last.

### 6. The Way We Live, and the Choices We Make Based on a Perceived "Reality"

Living a life fixated on illusion, fantasies, or "perceived" forms of reality can be dangerous, and lead to irreparable damage and issues later in life. This can be the result of a toxic relationship or marriage or making a poor monetary investment because of bad judgment that may lead to a scam or other loss that could have been avoided with some research and realistic expectations. We might hold on to friendships and relationships that offer little or no value to our lives, where we are led to believe and feel that other people have our best interests at heart when this is completely false. When this happens, it causes us to reevaluate everyone in our lives, fostering widespread distrust, which can impact healthy relationships as well.

Living in a world based on our own perceptions, and not the reality as it is, is a common occurrence that affects almost everyone to some degree. It's easy to say to someone with whom we disagree with that they are delusional or seeing something incorrectly because whether or not this is correct, we will likely view the same subject or situation in a way that is much different. If we share the same values and ideals with someone, we're likely to view from the same or similar perspective. Consider the definitions of reality versus reality:

**Reality:** the state or reality of what is and exists as it does in a material sense

**Perception:** the state of reflection of what we see or know from a mental perspective.

There is a lot of philosophical debate on what reality actually is, and whether it is defined by what we see and think, which can alter our universe and world as we know it, or is it always a skewed version of reality? If this is the case, we will never truly know the full meaning of what is or exists in its real form, if our sense is subject to mental and psychological bias. The way people, media, and organizations make impressions on us can also shift our perception of reality from one view to another. While philosophers may debate on the actual existence of reality, science defines what we see based cognitive process, and the ability to use rational thought and critical thinking to determine whether something we see or experience is real or different in how it Consider the following example:

Jennifer cycles to school daily. Her path includes taking a side road beside the downtown core of her small city. She often enjoys the view of the city center from afar, as it is usually too busy during the morning rush hour. One morning, she notices a large amount of smoke rising from several of the buildings. It appears devastating, and while she wants to look at it, she quickly heads to class, asking her friends if they were aware of it. Jennifer's perception is limited because she is can only see the smoke and thinks she might have spotted a few flames rising as well, which leads to panic. Later that day, she takes extra time to revisit downtown and discovers that the fire had been contained quickly and without as much damage as it, she thought it would cause. Her fear of fire, combined with a skewed view of what she thought was much worse, caused her perception to distort from reality. While she witnessed the incident first hand, her account was influenced by several factors, whereas someone on the opposite side of the affected buildings would have noticed a much different outcome.

In this case, the reality is exactly what has occurred, and while Jennifer's perception of the fire is correct, the magnitude and seriousness were embellished in her mind. When she reported her experience and asked about it at school, her concern about the incident, and whether anyone was injured, could have influenced how others may have interpreted the incident from a second-hand view. Realistically, the incident was less than newsworthy, as it was easily contained on a rooftop, with minimal damage and no casualties.

When someone or a group has the power to influence the way you think and/or manage your thoughts, this can gradually change the way you view a certain subject, and over time, may alter your opinions and/or beliefs. This has far more of an impact than one instance or another, but rather, it impacts an ongoing perception of many situations, including the people we interact with in life, and how we make decisions based on how outside factors influence and change our perspective.

### 7. How We See What We Believe: Finding the Truth Beneath the Surface

We see and believe what we want, especially when the reality is not an easy situation to face or confront. This often applies in abusive or manipulate relationships, where we want to view the abuser or toxic person as someone in a positive way and blame ourselves for their mistreatment towards us. Many people in an abusive situation will defend their partner, making statements like the following:

"If I only listened to him/her, they wouldn't have gotten angry with me."

"He/she won't do it again. I know they love me. I just need to try harder to please them, then everything will be ok."

"Next time won't be like this. They didn't mean to do it."

When living in a state of illusion or fantasy, your access to reality is available, though, through denial, you'll continue to live with the situation as it deteriorates over time. The risks involved in avoiding reality are grave, especially where violence and long-term mistreatment become the accepted norm, as these will worsen over time. Unfortunately, it often takes a major event or tragic event before reality is inescapable, and the only option is to peel back the surface and find the truth beneath. This is often a painful and difficult process and may require professional counseling and/or therapy to cope, where the situation creates an overhaul of your life, causing you to question everyone and everything.

How can you strip away the false, perceived realities and illusions, and focus on what's real? This may not be a difficult process in theory, but the emotional and psychological impact is significant, as it can be emotionally painful to look beneath a mask and find the ugly truth below. The following questions and ideas that can help you begin taking inventory of the relationship or situation you are in, to determine what is real and what needs to be further examined or questioned. For example, if you are in a toxic relationship, you may consider these points for analysis:

- Why statements do your partner make about you? Are they true and valid? When something is negatively said about us, the normal response would be to take defense and make a response, or simply ignore it. In an abusive relationship, we may dislike the statement, though it becomes internalized and, at some point, believed to be true. When this happens, and you reach the stage where you have compromised self-confidence, you may not give yourself the benefit of the doubt anymore, and continually discount your sense of worth to appease your partner. To take a closer, and honest look at your situation, you'll need to answer each question truthfully:

  - If your partner accuses you of being worthless, is this really true? Do you feel this way because of their accusation or because you truly feel this way?

  - If you feel worthless, has this always been an issue, having a lack of confidence, or is it something you've experienced with your current partner only?

- Does your partner value what you have to say and what you do for them, or is it never enough? Have their demands increased?

- Do you feel insecure about your appearance/intelligence/capabilities/self-worth? If yes, did your partner say anything to contribute to these feelings of worthlessness or feeling unimportant?

- If the relationship has since ended, have they tried to get in contact with you? What did they say and what impact did it have on you? Did they use guilt or make you feel this way during the contact?

These questions, and others that target your relationship, are not easy to ask yourself and can lead to uncomfortable results. You may experience inner conflict and consider bargaining with each answer, taking full or partial blame where it is unwarranted. In a toxic or abusive relationship, you'll notice a loss of identity as well, because the illusion or imagined ideal of the relationship is not what you're actually facing, and your partner will try everything within their power to undermine and control you. In a high control group or relationship, this will result in a modified personality, where you will behave and act in ways that benefit your partner while burying your own authentic self. After the relationship has ended, it will take a while to regain your sense of identity, as well as healing.

# Chapter 3: How Learning Psychology Can Help Us Recognize and Maintain our Identity

## 8.  Examples of Real vs. Perceived Realities

Who are we? The challenges of self-identity in a world fixated on labels and categories can be significant. Often, we are shaped by how we are raised and to what extent we are shaped into a socially acceptable version of ourselves. Sometimes, we identify by our career, our marital and/or parental status, our talents (artist, musician), or something easy to affix to ourselves. We often use simple labels because they are easy to identify with. Stereotypes, as damaging and harmful as they are in reality, have been used as labels in society, often discrimination and mistreatment will result.

In a world eager to judge and categorize people, it can be a challenge to truly know and understand who we are as individuals. We become comfortable with what or who we are, whether we identify with our political views, profession, or other quick one or two-word descriptions that have a preconceived idea or view of themselves. In labeling people this way, we cover over the real personality within. How do people identify themselves? What is the response when someone asks you who you are, or to explain a bit about yourself? Consider the two lists of definitions that can be used to describe yourself. Imagine you are in an interview, and you have the option of expressing anything and everything about you, without any restrictions or specifications, which types of characteristics or traits would you choose:

| Labels (close-ended descriptions) | Open descriptions that can be expanded upon |
|---|---|
| Career: lawyer, accountant, chef, customer service representative, sales clerk, etc. | Compassionate and determined (this leaves an opening to explore the subjects you are compassionate about and what determination you have to make the world a better place, for example.) |
| Husband/wife/partner, parent | Nurturing, caring, and non-judgmental. These descriptions |

| | |
|---|---|
| (mother/father, grandparent) or another familial role | can lead to more information on why and how you resemble these attributes. |
| Political party affiliation or registration | Activist for social justice and community organizations - this can lead to more information and description about the type of causes you feel strongly about, shedding light on how you view them and how/why you feel strongly |
| Artist, musician, writer | Creative, innovative, free-spirited. |

## 9.  Reality vs. Perceived Reality

In a world where we are constantly linked to online posts, news media, and second-hand reports, often differing from one source to another, it becomes difficult to determine what to believe and how we should view or assess information that we read or see. Unless we witness an incident unfold in front of us directly, we may not receive the same report from someone else who witnessed the same event. This is often due to the variance in perception from one person to another. This can occur where two people witness the exact same occurrence, though based on their previous experience and ideas of what was seen, their accounts will differ, at least slightly. Consider the following example:

Mandy is a cyclist who takes all the necessary precautions when traveling in the city to and from work. On the way to her office one morning, she witnesses to cars suddenly impact one another, resulting in serious injuries and damages. As she begins to see the event unfold, she is simultaneously watching the road and traffic lights to heed any warnings or change inflow. This event comes at a complete shock and causes her to pull over and take a few minutes. She remains on the scene, to see the outcome and answer any questions as a witness to the incident, to be of any help that she can.

Another witness to the incident is Jack, who is a former racecar driver, and has suffered some injuries in the past, though minor in comparison to other drivers. He's never nervous on the road and always remains calm, even when there is a traffic jam or accident. On the same day as the incident, Jack happened to be parked at an intersection where Mandy rode across on her bicycle, and just on the other side, he saw the collision. It happened quickly, and although he viewed the incident from a different angle than Mandy, he had a full and unobstructed view of the scene.

When Mandy and Jack are questioned about their experience with the accident, and what they witnessed, they may recount the event in different ways: Mandy might relate the incident as a traumatic event, as it occurred suddenly and without warning, while Jack may describe it in a less serious fashion, considering he is used to these occurrences and doesn't view this incident as earth-shattering and traumatic in the same way the Mandy does. Overall, both witnesses have the same story to tell, though if each of them was to relate their version to someone who wasn't present at the scene, the story would be slightly different. This is due to their change in perception and perspective. If you have a fear or phobia of a specific item or situation that plays a role in an incident, your reaction and explanation of the event may be far more severe and dramatic than someone with a significantly different view.

Reality is above all other levels of illusion, fantasy, and perception of reality. Real experience can be altered from one person to another, though overall, we know that what we see is a real event, and therefore it transcends and version or account of it that deviates from the accurate details. When someone asserts a perception of reality as a real danger, for example, then it can cause alarm when none is warranted. Consider a situation where a person has a fear of heights, and when they peek over the balcony of a tall high rise, they think they might fall. They may even forbid other people to venture near the balcony, stating the possibility of falling, even where there are safety devices and structures in place that would prevent an accident. In this situation, fear is the culprit that skews a reality (safe balcony) into an unsafe situation, based on the perception of danger.

Before you consider differentiating between reality and perception, consider that everything we view and experience is filtered through our own thoughts, emotions, and previous experience. In knowing this, we can take a step back and understand how one's mind can cloud or fog a standard, uneventful experience into something exhilarating or dangerous. Imagine if someone else viewed the same event on video, would they see exactly what we describe, or something different or less concerning? To separate our perception from reality, these steps can prove helpful and allow us to remove the filter or fog that changes our vision:

1. Consider a part of your life or a situation that you want or need to change, and determine why it is important to do so.

2. Figure out the causes(s) of this matter, and how deep the issue goes, as there may be a number of factors that contribute to this problem. For example, if you have financial struggles, you might attribute this to a lack of income, though if the problem persists after you have begun a new job with better pay, there may be other factors involved, such as financial

commitments, loan payments, unforeseen expenses and/or poor spending and saving habits.

3. When you delve into the contributing factors that may play a role in your situation, consider your thoughts during this process. Do any of these factors cause grief or anxiety? Is there an outstanding situation you need to face, but prefer to avoid it due to its unpleasantness?

4. Once you've thoroughly assessed your own thoughts and ideas, consider feedback from other people, and determine how they can help you find what might be contributing to a difficult situation. Often, another person's perception, while it might not be accurate, will be unbiased and focus on the situation and the causes of it, and without attaching your fears and/or emotions.

5. Once you have a compilation of factors and ideas from yourself and others with whom you've discussed the situation, take a careful look through them, and write or record them on a list for easy tracking. Make sure you take them

seriously and understand the importance of each item. Don't discount or dismiss any of the points; consider them equally, as part of a puzzle that will develop into a solution.

6. After you have given each point equal consideration, review them again with the intention of eliminating any items that are not relevant or least likely to be problematic or a contributing force to your issue. For example, if you find yourself struggling with someone at work due to a personality conflict, you may simply blame them for their behavior, without taking into consideration you and others may know. In an effort to improve the relationship, you might assess various factors, which may point to specific conditions or experiences the person is having that they are struggling with, and they do not have the emotional control to withhold their expressions around you and/or others. On the other hand, there may be no easy solution, though often we can find some factors that could be part of the root, and work on improving them as best as possible.

7.  Once you have refined the items that have the
    most impact on the situation, determine what
    next steps you need to take to minimize them
    and their impact on your life or the situation.

Taking these steps in order, and repeating some of the assessments and process of elimination, is a valuable tool in stripping away the cloud of perception that can lead to incorrect ideas and ineffective attempts to resolve matters.

# Chapter 4: How to Analyze People

## 10. Self Analysis: Understanding Yourself Before Analyzing Other People

Understanding and knowing about ourselves through self-analysis is vital to know more about who we are individually and how outside people, environment, and circumstances have an impact on us. Often, we may overlook or dismiss aspects of our personality and behavior that are picked up or readily noticed by someone, who may use this trait to either help or exploit us. Sometimes, we may try to understand or assess someone so know why they act or behave in a certain way, and how we can adjust to relate and/or communicate with them effectively. In some cases, spouses of abusive partners may attempt to understand a specific personality disorder, and whether it is an underlying reason for the abuse or toxic behavior. On the other hand, we might try to figure out how a person can be positive and ambitious despite experiencing setbacks in life, so that we may learn from them and understand their internal methods for coping and conquering their goals.

Before we can adequately evaluate someone else, it is vital to learn self-analysis. We need to become comfortable with our inner thoughts, emotions, and behavior, before we can assess someone else, as to how we communicate and act towards others, has an impact on them as well. When we review a situation where there is a conflict, we may immediately look at the other person(s) before considering our own role in the discussion, debate, or argument that resulted. Even if there is no fault of our own, it's important to rule out any influential markers or perceptions of us the other people may have had, such as a gesture or tone that could be misunderstood. For this reason, and to begin on a neutral level, begin the steps of self-analysis.

Self-analysis is defined as an internal evaluation of your own thoughts, behaviors, and resulting actions. It is a way to enhance self-care, by delving into our own thoughts and emotions, to gain a better understanding of ourselves. This can be done by following these steps:

1.  Think about yourself and how you view yourself. Consider all the negative, positive, and neutral attributes that you would attach to you. If you find that most of your attributes of this analysis shift towards the negative, you may be

too critical or hard on yourself, whereas if there are many positive traits you can think of in yourself, this is a sign of confidence. Neutral and/or a balance of everything may be a balance of acknowledging what you are good at and finding areas for improvement. Overall, you should gauge your own self-perception and determine what that is and whether it's positive or negative.

2. Consider other people's feedback, and be sure to ask a variety of people, not just those who are critical in general, or anyone who would shy away from being honest and upfront. You could ask them to assess their thoughts of you in a constructive way, looking for points of improvement along with positive traits. It's best to obtain a cross-section of different people and opinions, with little or no coaching, so the results are more honest and useful.

3. When you receive the feedback, consider that not all terms are necessarily completely negative or positive, depending on the person who uses the term to describe you. For example, independence is often seen as a positive trait,

though to some people, it is seen as less collaborative and team-oriented, which may be useful in certain work and organizational environments. Some people may consider a competitive nature healthy and natural, while others see it as negative in certain situations. Some attributes are always well regarded, such as reliability, fairness, and innovation, whereas others tend to be vastly regarded as negative: arrogant, ill-tempered, and indecisive. Aggression may be frowned upon in situations where patience and care are needed, whereas an abrasive environment may accept, even embrace some forms of perceived aggression as a sign of strength, even where it is not.

4. Once you have collected all the feedback, and have a good list of attributes to work with, build a list or table and move each of the items under their appropriate category:

    a. Which items are considered valuable skills, characteristics, and abilities? These may include a sense of responsibility or accountability, diligence, honesty, hard-working and reliable

b. Do you have hobbies and areas of expertise that help you develop? Do you play an instrument, speak more than one language, enjoy reading, sports, or an artistic pursuit?

c. How would I describe my relationship with family, friends, neighbors, and colleagues?

d. What goals do you have currently, and what milestones are you looking to achieve?

e. What are my areas of improvement?

There are some key benefits from self-assessment, which include the following:

- Self-criticism, in a constructive way. When you assess your feelings, actions, and behaviors, your perspective moves outside, as you look within. Often, we can be critical about ourselves, which can be habitual, though constructive criticism can give us a balanced view of what we can improve upon, to reduce what we're not content with

- Receiving constructive feedback from others is of great benefit, and allows us to see who we are from the outside, without going through the effort of attempting this ourselves. Contrary to what many people think, others may have a more favorable view of you, offering some new ideas and advice that can serve as a benefit to self-improvement.

- The combination of feedback and self-perception creates a wide view, or 360 degrees of perspectives, which can paint a full picture of reflection.

- There is a potential to build confidence. When we take the approach of self-assessment, this can become part of a self-care pattern, where we aim to take care and improve ourselves together.

Gaining a fuller perspective of who we are, what we experience, and the world around us is a valuable way to achieve a greater understanding of reality by viewing our world through several lenses and viewpoints. Once we are cognizant of our own perception and how it may differ from reality, we can take a more pragmatic approach to experiences in life, and how we make decisions.

## 11. Techniques on Analysis: How it is Done?

**Reading People, Observing Body Language, Various Methods of Communication and Cues**

Reading people and analyzing their behavior is an important tool for understanding their cues and various reasons for acting in certain ways. Looking for cues is not difficult, and many signs can be picked up in body language, positioning, and other non-verbal expressions.

**Close Proximity/Positioning:**

When you first meet someone, most people will allow a reasonable amount of personal space between you and them. The average personal space allowance is about eighteen inches, or close to this distance. If you ride subway trains or other means of public transportation that require close contact with other people, you notice how most will try to maintain a space of at least a few inches in between them and others, for safety and security. Most people will offer a handshake, though an embrace is often reserved for people you know more intimately, or work with closely. If someone you first meet trues to close or minimize the gap between you and them at an early stage in your relationship, it may be a sign they feel comfortable and want to foster that connection. This can also be a sign that a person you've only just met to gauge how close they can get to you and how far you will let them. They will observe your reaction, and whether you welcome their close contact or feel intimidated by it. When this happens, it can be a manipulator's way to learn your comfort zone and what they can and cannot get away with. If you find yourself in a situation where someone is trying to get too familiar too fast, consider it a warning sign, or at least a situation to monitor, for your own safety.

**Hand Gestures:**

People who strive for control tend to rub their hands together, or their neck with their hands. This can be a clear indication in some people, though it may also signal that a manipulative person feels guilty or anxious about what they're going to do. Consider how some people get sweaty palms when they tell a lie or perform a dishonest act. They may also react this way when they are about to try a manipulative tactic or trickery and may feel conflicted about it. Other people who are more skilled in persuasion may not exhibit these symptoms, because they are well practiced, and no longer feel uneasy about their actions.

Another hand gesture that is common among manipulators is when the fingers are spread, with the tips outstretched, forming a tent. This is usually done while they are sitting, with their hands formed this way on a table or over their lap. This can signal a strong urge to achieve and maintain control over people and/or situations.

**Eye Contact:**

When eye contact is maintained, this means you are being taken seriously and listened to. There may be many reasons for why keen attention is being paid to you, and what you say, especially when someone has a reason to know more information: they may be trying to assist you for your own benefit, or learn something new. If someone is manipulative, they may be listening for cues or signs of inadequacies that they can use against you. Shifting eye movements or avoidance can indicate a lack of interest or occur due to distraction.

Generally, bodily movements than impede on your space or make you feel uncomfortable are often used by people who want to establish control. It is their way of invading your space physically and making you feel as though they are powerful. When a manipulator does this, they often look for cues from you: do you shrink back and try to avoid their covering nature, or do you stand firm to them and assert yourself? Someone looking for easy "prey" may be easier to target, but only if they are receptive to the manipulative techniques. For example, a salesperson may be eager to close a sale, and in their determination, they use favorable language towards the potential customers, highlighting the benefits of the item they are selling. In doing so, they may create an extended comfort zone, where the customer feels obliged to allow them to continue speaking to them. They may touch your arm or pat you on the back, as a friend would, gauging how receptive you are to their closeness. For some people, these actions make them feel "trapped" as if they need to commit to the sale, where others may feel compelled to buy into the "benefits" of becoming a consumer. Where a salesperson is crafty, but careful in their tactics, they may be able to sell to someone who doesn't really want to buy the product, but does so because of pressure. In this way, persuasion moves into a stronger form of manipulation.

### 12. What Do Manipulators Look for in Their Targets?

There are specific non-verbal cues and gestures that manipulators look for when they target people. Some skills levels are advanced enough that they can pick up from minor or subtle gestures, which you may have no control over, or notice yourself. The following non-verbal cues are often noticed by people looking to assess you and determine how likely you are to fall under their "spell":

- Fidgeting with your hands and shaky hands is a sign of nervousness and anxiety. A person fidgeting may simply be nervous because they are meeting someone for the first time, or preparing or a public speech. When someone with ill intentions notices this, they will know or assume that you may react this way often around certain people and/or situations. This places them in a slightly more advantageous situation if they notice you are easier to influence in this state. For example, if someone is about to give a speech to a large crowd, and displays signs of nervousness, a manipulator may play the role of the reassuring friend, comforting you and "building" your confidence, so you feel better about your presentation so that you begin to trust them and see their actions as sincere. This may be part of their overall techniques to convince you of their good intentions, which are not altruistic.

- Avoiding eye contact is another sign of nervousness or fear. Some people will avoid looking in the direction of an event or person who is offensive or causing them grief. This will be noticed by someone who is manipulative and show them exactly how you react to unpleasantness, and which items or situations cause you to react in this way. A manipulative person will want to learn your fears: what paralyzes you to the point of doing whatever it takes to avoid a specific situation or scenario? If they are capable of mimicking a situation that makes you uncomfortable, you are more likely to comply with their demands.

- Posture speaks a lot about a person's self-confidence and how they feel about themselves. A person who slouches forward may suffer from low self-esteem and appear to be apologetic or feel unworthy. When they receive positive attention and feedback, the effects are sudden and surprising. They may begin to feel liked and accepted by someone, even a manipulator, without realizing the feedback can easily switch to criticism or bullying. If they stand tall and look confident, some manipulative people may not focus on them if they appear to be mentally and emotionally strong already; however, some manipulators will view them as a challenge and gladly take it on, so they can find out what makes the person so confident.

When someone is looking for a target to take advantage of and manipulate, they will often look for signs in you that indicate it's easy to gain control, either immediately, or in time. A skilled manipulator will take their time if their goal is to secure a relationship or business connection with someone they see as a benefit to their life: this could involve money, status, and/or connections to other people in the community. A narcissist will expect that someone they manipulate will be receptive to their every need, and will use flattery to boost your confidence while tearing you down later when and if you don't give them what they want.

Keeping an eye on your body movements and gestures is an important way to set boundaries and establish a comfort zone while signaling to anyone who may be manipulative that you are not going to fall for their tactics. This can be done by using some of the following techniques, even if you don't always feel confident or secure, you can make a few simple changes to avoid the onset of manipulation:

- If someone steps too close, too fast, you can simply step back. If this happens again, and they don't heed the warning, place your hand in front to signal, "that's enough, I'll stand here, you stay there" as a means of non-verbal conversation. Any attempts to ignore this gesture should be considered on purpose and an attempt to gain control over you. If you feel physically threatened, leave the area immediately and avoid contact with the person completely.

- Maintain eye contact and watch for their reaction. Are they keen on setting their eyes on you as well, as a means to challenge you, or are they making a meaningful connection? This can be difficult to determine unless you know the person well. For people who are typically controlling, they will look to notice how much attention you pay to them. By showing that you are observing them, you are letting them know that you are paying attention. This may keep them on alert, and they may back away, or see the eye contact as a challenge to try a method of persuasion.

- Keep your posture strong and firm. Stand or sit upright with your shoulders back. This will demonstrate that you are comfortable and confident with yourself. Even if you don't necessarily feel this way at times, it can be a valuable way to discourage certain malignant types of people who prey on those they see as vulnerable or weak.

- Shake hands strong and firm, without squeezing the hand too much or appearing too aggressive or avoidant. A firm, yet brief handshake is enough to state that you expect a fair, honest connection, without any room for persuasion tactics. A manipulator may still find a way to use one of their techniques, though if you maintain a similar disposition and stance as the handshake, keeping it straight-forward and fair, there is little room for them to succeed with their sly attempts to control you.

Always keep an eye on behavior or gestures that make you question the other person and their intentions. While some people may be simply nervous or fidgety at times, even as a habit, a manipulative person will usually appear cool and calm, and may only appear slightly nervous anticipating their next move. Generally, narcissists and sociopaths tend to hold their composure when they use manipulative tactics, causing other people to build confidence in them; if they appear confident and sure of themselves, they may also seem more trustworthy than they are. For this reason, it's best to keep an eye on behavior that triggers your doubts and concerns, as there may be a good reason to feel this way.

# Chapter 5: Brainwashing and Subconscious Mind Control

## 13. What is Brainwashing and Mind Control?

Brainwashing and mind control are terms often used to describe the systematic, manipulative, and sometimes subtle methods to coerce, condition and alter the mind's way of thinking. This impacts the cognitive processes in the mind, which impact behavior and perception. Often, mind control techniques are not immediately recognized because they happen over time, and can be gradual, where our thinking patterns and cognitive processes alter over a period of time, not at once. Many different people and groups apply this form of mind control, from politicians, corporations, certain organizations (government or private), and cults or high control groups. While extreme forms of brainwashing involve physical and/or mental imprisonment, restricting freedom of choice and expression, while forcing an idealized set of rules and controlling thought patterns, there are many milder, common mind control techniques that occur today as well. We may not be aware of their effects until months, or years later, when we notice major changes have occurred and patterns in their life, including their relationships with family and friends, have changed.

When most people think of brainwashing, they may consider cults as one of the key ways in which brainwashing or mind control is developed, either corporate (pyramid schemes) or religion-based groups. Cults are also referred to high control groups and can often be less obvious and extreme at first, with their insidious intentions taking hold once they have a greater hold or level of control over the people that join and follow them. Similar tactics are used by individuals who fit one or more of the dark triad personalities, which are often unnoticed at first. The stages of using mind control techniques to manipulate and alter a person or group of people's way of thinking can be experienced by people of all backgrounds and ways of life. There are some common myths about brainwashing and the susceptibility of people to fall prey to these malicious techniques:

**Myth 1: Victims of brainwashing and mind control are less intelligent and more gullible than other people.**

This is inaccurate because many people with good education and intellect can be lured into a cult or similar organization for a variety of reasons. They may be lonely and bored, looking to join a group or organization that will help them socialize. They may be falsely led to believe they are joining as a volunteer to help the community in some way, or feel compelled to join a group because they have an interesting philosophy. In some situations, there are people who may be gullible in that they believe most people are capable of goodness, including a high control group. They may be impressed with their sense of community and inclusivity, which draws them to join. Even once they begin to question their teachings or beliefs, they may remain in the group to keep in touch with the other adherents.

**Myth 2: It's easy to figure out if you've joined a cult because their tactics are obvious.**

This could not be further from the reality of what happens when people join or entertain the idea of becoming part of a high control group. Some organizations and companies, such as pyramid schemes, may disguise their purpose as a self-improvement group with the purpose of giving you the tools to make better decisions in your life. If a person has grappled with financial strain, or they have a desire to improve their diet and way of living, a group that appears to promote healthy supplements and a means to earn extra income can appear attractive. Religious cults and pyramid schemes are masters at making new and curious people feel welcome and entitled when they attend meetings and/or seminars. They may become fast friends, treating you like royalty, and while this may seem unusual for some people, it's a welcome attitude that many other people will enjoy, especially if they lack personal relationships in life. These signs, while they are symptoms of a high control group, this won't necessarily be apparent to someone new who has little or no experience with these types of groups.

**Myth 3: People can guard themselves 100% from cults and highly controlling people and groups.**

While there are some truth and validity to this, there is no complete guarantee that any one method or another will completely protect you or someone you love from joining a cult. Fortunately, many people realize something is unusual or suspect within a short period of time, though some will continue to remain a member of the group because they have created new connections and friendships within and feel obliged to stay. This is a form of manipulation, also known as emotional blackmail, which is used in many cults. When a person initially joins, they are overwhelmed with personal attention and kindness, also known as "love bombing". Once they become a member and begin to comply and live like the others, they will eventually find that any deviation from their rules or questioning them, can lead to being expelled and ignored or shunned completely.

## 14. How to Determine if Someone is Using Manipulation and Mind Control on You

There are signs of manipulation, which can be detected from individuals and/or groups of people who are trying to convince you of a better option or life other than the one you currently live. Their tactics can be subtle by starting a friendship and getting to know more about you. What appears to be a real friendship forming is actually part of their plan: they are looking to know you well enough to determine your fears and weaknesses. They'll know if you hold certain values or ideals, whether you are susceptible to their influence and suggestions. A manipulative person will also make an impression on you in such a way that you won't necessarily notice, while at the same time, you'll begin picking up on their hints or suggestions as a part of the controlling process.

Once a manipulator feels comfortable with you and establishes what they can get away with, they will make an effort to control more of your life. Often, we are unaware of the early signs because we enjoy the positive side or perception of the person. Our perception fools us, clouding our vision so that we don't notice to maliciousness beneath. Recognizing the signs and guarding yourself against further abuse is the only way to safeguard yourself from emotional, psychological, and possibly physical harm. The following early signs provide a strong reason to question the validity of a person who shows interest in you:

- They will attempt to confine you either within a physical space and/or by limiting your connection and communication with friends and family. By doing this, they can exert greater control over you and your habits. For example, they may call you to find out where you are, even if you've just left work and commuting home, or expect you to spend more time with them than anyone else. Once they become comfortable with these restrictions, they will continue to monitor and control everything you do, though, in the beginning, signs will appear subtle. Be cautious about numerous texts, excessive contact, and wanting to know your location, whether this is infrequent or more often.

- A manipulator may appear to be a good listener, which is why they can be alluring and appreciated; however, they are listening for a specific reason: to learn your weaknesses and how to use them against you. This is a tactic used in sales and certain business relationships, where they analyze where they can focus on a specific need or want. For example, upon discovering that someone likes to gamble, and often fall into the habit of excessive betting, a manipulator may entice them with an investment offer or something risky that may appeal to them.

- They will alter their tone of voice to become loud and angry, which is an attempt to regain control over someone by use of fear. On the other hand, they can be passive-aggressive, and employ the silent treatment to punish their partner, making them feel as though they did something wrong that they must correct or feel guilty for. The silent treatment can be hurtful, as it feels as though love and care have been completely stripped away, forcing the target or victim to conform to a specific behavior or action in order to "restore" contact with the manipulator.

- A manipulator will become pushy, bringing up a situation or decision that must be made within a short period of time. They may have already known about the situation and the need for a decision in advance, though only release the information close to the deadline, to make you squirm and more prone to their power over you. In a panic, you might make a decision that is more aligned with what they want.

- They are judgmental and critical, and not in a constructive way. They will try to control every aspect of your life by dictating what you wear, how you act, and behave. They may try to seize power over your financial affairs, claiming they are an expert with money or insult your appearance if you don't dress or style your look as they prefer. In the early part of a relationship, they will compliment you excessively, to the point of non-stop flattery, and while it may seem over the top, it feels good and enjoyable to receive positive comments. Once they know the effect their words have on you, they can easily switch to a critical tone, until they see the desired changes in you. If you confront them about this behavior, they might excuse it as they want to help you improve somehow, or that your appearance and well-being is their primary concern, which is false.

- A manipulative person will play ignorant, even when they have knowledge about a certain subject or situation. This can be a frustrating experience, especially when it initially happens, and you know they are using this tactic to prolong a specific task or responsibility they must fulfill. By pretending not to know about it, they can buy themselves time, and cause other people to second guess what they really know. It can be used effectively with gaslighting, where a manipulator will convince you that anything you question them about is imagined or inaccurate, making you appear unstable.

- They often play the victim and will hold either you or someone else responsible for their misdeeds, even blaming their spouse for having an affair, when they are the ones at fault. A manipulator will gradually work this tactic into a relationship, but only when it suits their needs. Outside of this tactic, they will act strong and confident, and not victimized at all, which is a sign they are using this as a form of manipulation.

- Negative emotions are often displayed when it suits the manipulator. If they don't want you to be happy or satisfied in your life, they will do what it takes to make you feel less. They might accuse you of not giving them enough attention and threaten to leave when in reality, they are trying to keep you in a position of uncertainty and low self-esteem. Crying, yelling or acting depressed are all false emotions they will exhibit to evoke emotions and use them against you. For example, if they cry, you may second guess past negative experiences, and give them another chance. They will often use their own emotions (often exaggerated or false) to control how you feel and react.

Establishing and maintaining boundaries early in the relationship is key to protecting yourself from manipulation and any form of persuasion that can escalate into manipulative actions. If someone moves into your life too quickly and easily, it's often a sure sign that they are looking to establish control at some point, either soon or over time, and will use anything they can find against you. If they make promises too or try to get your signature on a contract immediately, this is a sign they are looking for you to commit to them without them doing the same in return. This can be dangerous, especially in situations where a lot of money is at stake, and the risk falls on the target or person the manipulator convinces to sign. Long-term relationships where abuse and mistreatment are common among toxic people, who will use and discard others as they see fit, often crushing other people's expectations for true love and honesty. The more you detect suspicious and questionable behavior early, the better your chances are for avoiding a heartbreaking situation later.

# Chapter 6: Manipulation and Persuasion

## 15. What is Manipulation and Persuasion and How to Recognize Them

We've all been the target of persuasion at some point in life, whether someone is trying to convince us to join them for an evening with friends at the theatre, even when you're not up to it, convincing you to try new food, fashion statement or product. Persuasion is often used in sales and sometimes by someone you know who is trying to convince you that a certain type of product or service is worth trying, even if just once. While persuasion can be persistent, often with one person pursuing another until they finally agree to "give it a try", it is generally harmless and serves no purpose other than to open the other person's mind to a new and/or different possibility than they may have imagined on their own. The close friend who coaxes you to try a new roller coaster with them, or tries a new restaurant in town are examples of persuasion.

Manipulation differs from persuasion because it doesn't serve any purpose other than to satisfy the manipulator, with no benefit to the person they are targeting. When a person uses persuasion, they often do so with the other person's well-being and benefit in mind. They may consider that a different choice in color for a new jacket or a change in fashion might be of benefit to the other person. The act itself would have no benefit to the person doing the persuading. For this reason, the person being persuaded might consider the advice if it is going to be an improvement or perceived to be. In fact, persuasion can be a selfless act, if the benefit of the change falls onto the person who makes the change.

## 16. The Difference Between Manipulation and Persuasion

How is manipulation different from persuasion? Manipulation serves the person who is trying to control someone else's actions or behavior in a way that benefits the manipulator, often through skillful words or techniques, to make the process more effective. This can be seen in schemes where a lot of convincing, even unethical practices, are used to talk someone into buying something they don't need or making an investment that will help the manipulator benefit, without consideration for the other person. Consider the following characteristics that separate the intentions of manipulation and persuasion:

| *Persuasion* | *Manipulation* |
| --- | --- |
| There is no intention in taking advantage of someone or trying to fool them into doing something harmful. The reason for persuasion can be benign and thoughtful, often placing the other person's interests ahead. | The intention may involve fooling or tricking the other person into believing they will receive a reward or other benefit in buying or signing up for something so that the manipulator stands to benefit from the transaction or action. |
| There's no | Manipulation often involves |

| hidden agenda or ill-intentioned reason for persuasion. The entire process is fair and transparent | hiding certain outcomes or aspects of the decision that could detrimental, leaving little or no transparency. |
|---|---|
| The person being persuaded may likely benefit, or at the very least, the outcome will be neutral or minimal. | There may be something to lose from allowing someone to manipulate you into signing a contract for a service you don't need, costing your money that you shouldn't spend, while the manipulator stands to benefit from your loss |
| There is nothing to hide, as the intention | There is often something to hide or conceal because the intention is not altruistic in |

| is good | nature. |
| --- | --- |
|  |  |

A person can be ethically persuaded, because often they may already lean in favor of complying with the suggestion or idea that the other person is offering. For example, they may be in the market for a new vehicle or appliance, and a good friend or colleague may recommend, by way of persuasion, a preferred brand or model. They will likely persuade you because they have personal and positive experience themselves, that they would like to see you benefit from. A manipulator, on the other hand, will try to sell you something less efficient, even damaged, at full cost, and not reveal any deficiencies. Unless their vile methods are discovered, they may be successful in cheating someone and doing so without any remorse.

## 17. Preventing Yourself From Abuse

There are techniques you can use in your life to prevent the likelihood that you will be targeted for abuse and exploitation. It's important to realize that not all tactics used are obvious, and some are very subtle, almost undetectable until they worsen over time. Preventing the impact of abuse may not be easy where the person is cunning in their manipulative techniques. For this reason, it's vital to keep an eye on the early signs that will emerge quickly and occur fairly often in a situation where the goal is to win you over, so that you can be prepared and baited for further control. The following signs are important to pay attention to, as they occur fairly early in the relationship with a person or in the beginning stages of joining a high control group. The fact that these early warning signs are easy to detect and similar for individuals, as well as groups, should be kept in mind, as they often apply to all forms or tactics used in dark psychology:

**Love Bombing**

When you first meet someone, do you feel as though they are too perfect or unlikely to be as good as they appear to be? They may claim to be your soulmate or express that you're like no one they've met before, or that you're the perfect match for them. This is also a common trait in high control groups, where new members are welcomed with open arms and a sudden burst of love and connection is fused, making them feel as though they've found the perfect new group of friends. This tactic is known as "love bombing", and is used bait to make people feel as though they are accepted and belong as they are. This is a powerful tool in convincing people that they are a part of something greater than themselves and instills a sense of duty or obligation, so they simply join and follow the rules without question. In a relationship, the same tactic is used by showing continuous and sometimes extensive flattery and adoration, making a person feel special and loved when in reality, the tactic will wear off in time, once the control is established.

**Control of Association, Activities, and Thinking**

Once you join a cult or high control group, you'll notice that they will have introduced you to a set of rules or guidelines they expect you to follow, without question. They may ask you to spend more time with group members, partake in certain ceremonies or events, which in itself, can fill up your schedule, taking you away from family and friendships that value. They may encourage you to find other people to join and share their message or teachings. The level of control can go as far as dictating personal appearance, thought patterns and with whom you are allowed to associate. These are dangerous changes and can impact many aspects of your life. Any disobedience or questioning of their rules can lead to punishment, where other members who have extended their "love" to you now ignore or treat you indifferently. This will only become restored if you return to their ways, even at the loss of your own family and friends.

At first, you may see the changes in how you think and associate with people as something positive and empowering. You may believe or buy into their ideals of self-improvement and follow them diligently. This is where they "sell" you on their way of life and convince you to adhere to their principles and actions. This is a powerful and deceitful way to gain someone's trust, even though the use of fear and making someone feel incomplete without the group of people involved. You may try to convince friends and/or family to join an organization or cult because you feel compelled to "save" them, just as other adherents felt when they recruited you. Anyone who questions the high control group's teachings, even before joining, could become blacklisted. If you express that family or friends are resistant to getting involved, you may be expected to break off contact with them. This is where a cult or manipulative group may convince you that you're better off without family, and you can thrive with their organization instead, reaching a higher level of existence and satisfaction in life.

Your own thinking techniques will change significantly after you become involved with a cult of a high control group. You might notice that your level of tolerance isn't what it used to be, and you might have adopted some of the manipulative techniques used on yourself to recruit others. In time, you develop a sense of dependency on them for validation and self-worth, so that any unapproved gestures or comments you make are expediently dealt with through their own conditioning process, either by punishing you with silent treatment or forcing you to make amends in one way or another. This is a powerful way to keep you in line with their control while keeping you away from outside family, friends, and connections.

**Using Their Own Language and Terms**

Cults and high control groups often develop their own terminology or re-define words to create a loaded language. The reasons for changing the meaning of some words to their own allows them to use language as a means to stop the thinking process among their followers and convince them that they have all that is needed within the organization. For example, if a high control group expects their followers to engage in heavy labor or proselytize for hours on end, they will rebrand the word "freedom" to fit in with their way of life, even where it is one of coercion and control. Any mention of the word freedom will swiftly connect followers to their cult's definition of it, and this will convince them to continue the onerous work, even to their own detriment and loss of health. Many people will invest in pyramid schemes, convinced they would reap major success, only to be at a loss many months or years later. Instead of viewing the business for the financial trap it is, they will have been taught to see it as a "business opportunity" or a lucrative means to start your own business, all of which is completely fabricated.

How can you avoid cults, high control groups, and organizations that are malignant?

There are some signs to look for, which can be seen very early in your exchange with someone who is trying to recruit you and others:

- Any questions you ask are met with vague answers because they don't have the solutions they propose, only a means to convince you that they do. If you decide to join, questioning any of their teachings will be forbidden or highly discouraged, which is a sign that their organization is controlling and dangerous.

- They appear happy and friendly to the point of excessiveness and offer compliments and flattery to get your attention. This is a technique that is used by narcissists as well, to gain the trust of others, and make sure they can make a strong impression that you won't forget. This will entice you to reconnect with them at a later time and listen to what they have to say because the initial connection was satisfying. Unfortunately, everything said is false and crafted solely with the purpose of recruitment. Knowing this in advance will save you a lot of grief later.

- They have the answers to everything, but none at all. As mentioned in the first point: if you ask any questions, you'll receive no concrete answers, only reassurance that they

have the ultimate way of life. They may
pretend to know everything because they
have a certain advantage of being a part of
the organization or high control group. This
also gives the impression that they belong to
an elite or exclusive group, and by inviting
you, they are extending their privilege to you.

- Words will take on a new definition that
  becomes a loaded language that changes
  what they truly mean to a completely new
  concept. Words like "family", "love", and
  "freedom" are examples that have been
  misused in this way, leading their adherents
  to believe, by word association and re-
  definition, that by joining a cult, they have
  achieved a better way of life. Because there is
  no allowance or tolerance for questioning
  their system of teachings, and harsh
  punishments for people who do, including
  ex-communication, it becomes easier to
  accept the restrictions of life and language.

Other forms of control are used when you join a high
control group, which becomes apparent more over
time when you have more to lose and feel invested in

their cause. It's important to realize that while high control groups are successful at recruiting people, they often fail at keeping their followers for long periods of time. Many new recruits are born into the organization and experience the pressure to remain a member, because of family and friends staying inside. New recruits don't have as much to lose, though if they become intimately involved with someone or feel that the organization serves a greater purpose, through successful brainwashing and ongoing conditioning, it can be difficult for them to leave. The best way to inoculate yourself against cult mind control is to always remain aware and remove yourself from situations that make you uncomfortable right away. There are specific techniques used in schemes, cults and powerful individuals to persuade, often with detrimental results, through a process known as NLP (neuro-linguistic programming). This is explored in-depth in chapter 8.

# Chapter 7: Controlling Your Own Mind

## 18. How to Guard Yourself against Exploitation

How do you know if you may be a target for the next scheme or considered as bait for someone's manipulative tactics? Until we are met with a situation that can be manipulative and exploitive in nature, we won't know until we are faced with the scenario of how we will think and what the specific tactics will be. When this happens, it's important to be prepared and ready to take steps to guard and protect your life and any decisions that you might make that can negatively impact you and the people in your life. What are the signs we should look for to determine whether a situation is a potential pitfall that we should avoid?

- Are the person or people involved appealing to your weakness (or perceived weakness), and do they use this as a motivation or basis to convince you to believe in something or buy a specific product? An example might be to mention statistics on home invasions or instill a certain fear that this might happen, to convince someone to buy an expensive home security system, when there is no need for one, and no initial intention of buying one.

- What you gain from the situation versus what the other person gains from it. This is a key piece that should be used to evaluate any potential for fraud or other scenarios that can have a negative impact on your life. If the situation doesn't involve money or sales, it could be a relative or friend who has a hidden agenda and wishes to use you or something you do against another person for their own benefit. For example, they may want you to take sides with them against someone when there is no reason to do so, and in doing this, you risk further family division. In some cases, there may be legitimate reasons for taking aside, though, in everyday or small disputes, it's often not worth the drama and emotional upset that results later.

- Is the person or group of people isolating you from other people? This may not too obvious in the early stages or a sign at all until you become more familiar and attached to them. When he happens, you may find that you're encouraged to attend certain events and connect with specific people already involved in the high control group. In a relationship scenario, you may notice frequent calls to check up on you, which can become obsessive in nature. This can lead to the person or group expecting you to join and associate with them on an increasingly frequent basis while becoming irritating or disapproving of your friends and family. In this way, they are attempting to control your contact with others, so that you lose the support and security, and as a result, becomes more vulnerable and easier to control and influence.

- A manipulative person will be moody and emotionally unhinged at times when they don't get what they want. This symptom may appear minimal at first, and appear as though they are having a bad day, and causing you to question your own methods.

- How do you feel when you are around the person or group? Do you notice rising anxiety or stress when you are with them or anticipate seeing them? You may feel concerned about disappointing them and strive to do more to win their favor. This can occur without fully understanding the reasons why, because the tactics are used in such a way that you feel as though you are doing it out of your own free will without any coercion or control.

Knowing what to look for is the first line of defense in protecting yourself from dangerous people and groups that will try to manipulate you for their own benefit. Keeping yourself a reasonable distance from people you don't know well is one of the best ways to maintain a safe boundary, and this applies to emotional and psychological boundaries as well. At any time, if a person makes you feel inadequate or that you need them for something, consider it a warning sign and take precautions early, to dodge their techniques.

### 19. Knowing Your Vulnerabilities

In order to prepare ourselves with the tools we need to guard our best interests in life and avoid the potential for manipulation and exploitation, it's important that we learn and embrace our own vulnerable nature and weaknesses. A weakness shouldn't be dismissed as unimportant, nor should we see it as a character flaw or negative. Every single person has a vulnerability, and more than one, whether we know it or not, or recognize them. If we don't find a weakness within ourselves, we haven't looked deep within, as everyone shares at least several. Vulnerabilities are synonymous with being human and knowing that while we have a lot of strengths and skills, we have areas that are not as well developed or conquered yet. In this way, we can look at our vulnerabilities as something that we should guard and take care of, as exposing them to the wrong person or people can ignite their sense of taking advantage of us.

A manipulator will seek out a vulnerable person, or someone with a perceived weakness as their preferred target. If they don't choose you, this means they haven't found a vulnerability to attack, nor do they see something they want. For example, some people might target someone who has experienced a recent loss, because they see an opportunity to exploit someone who is suffering a tragedy, and may not use critical thinking and evaluation to identify the malice nature of the true intent. When this happens, it can be devastating in cases where money and/or investments are stolen, or people are coerced into buying something they have no use for, though trusted the person enough because they seemed kind and genuine. For other people, having a quite or passive demeanor can bait them for people who are aggressive and see easy prey.

How can knowing our vulnerabilities help us avoid the pitfalls of manipulation? If we understand what we are afraid of, or how we appear to others, we might have a better idea of what draws certain people and their plans to exploit our way. You may want to consider some of the following attributes, while not considered weaknesses, they are often perceived to be, and this can cause a manipulator to target you as a result:

- You may be seen or known as a friendly, accepting person that often says "yes". This doesn't mean you are always agreeable, but the appearance of being so can flag someone's attention as "as to manipulate"

- You're quite and keep to yourself, which may be perceived as shyness or having a fear of social situations.

- You need validation from your peers, and often copy or follow everything they do. Your outward attitude and disposition may be positive, though internally, you struggle with self-esteem and feel inadequate until someone shows approval.

- There may be circumstances in your life, such as a loss of a loved one, a loss of belonging in a storm or fire, or other severe circumstances that put you at risk of fraudulent activity.

As you assess your own weaknesses, look for the items or characteristics that you feel are likely to be targeted. Chances are, you may have already encountered people or situations that cause you to reflect on your perceived weaknesses. This can give you a good insight into what others see, and how you can manage your interaction with them. Asking for feedback or ideas from close family and friends can also help you to determine what others may see in you that can encourage certain forms of exploitation and manipulation.

**When People Exploit Weaknesses to Create Emotional Dependence: How They Train You to**

## Accept and Support Them Without Resistance, to your Own Detriment

One of the first methods manipulative people use to control others is by observing them and determining what their weaknesses are. To be clear, a toxic, manipulative person defines weakness as something they can use against you, and should not be considered a character flaw. For example, having compassion for animals or raising a young family may be viewed as a vulnerability or weakness, because you have a commitment to animals and people. You may have certain struggles, as anyone else can experience, though a person with an agenda to control you and others will use anything that you hold with value or with passion as an object they can use against you. This is because they are narcissistic in nature, and likely sociopathic, which are included in the dark triad of malignant and dangerous personality disorders. They do not view you as a human being, but rather a subject they can use to their advantage for their own pleasure or benefit, often for sex, money or improving their status.

A manipulator will train you to accept their mistreatment and abuse of you gradually so that it becomes increasingly more difficult to determine what is happening. You might not realize the impact they have on your health and well-being until much later, when you've experienced their worst, and can no longer take it. Often, they will discard you once they obtain what they want, leaving you to question your own actions or faults, none of which have anything to do with their malignant activity. On the other hand, a manipulator may become attached or obsessed with you, tracking your every move and know more about you than they should. This can progress once you become relaxed with them, and convinced they are altruistic and good in their motives. Once you realize the detriment they can and will cause, you may choose to distance yourself, only to find they won't accept the rejection, which can lead to further damage:

- They will attempt to smear your name and reputation within the community, as a way to punish you for leaving them and no longer doing everything they want.

- A narcissist or dark triad personality will use people against you, if they have an alliance with them, or try to convince them to take their side, in the case of a divorce or dissolving a business agreement or arrangement you may have had with them.

- They may try taking you to court over child custody, if this is a relevant issue following a breakup, and withhold support payments or other financial arrangements, even if ordered by the court, just out of spite.

A dark triad personality will never allow you to leave their grip of control easily. In fact, leaving them can result in far more danger, especially if they have a history of violence and criminal activity. They view you as belonging to them, and they will stop at nothing to convince you to return under their influence, usually by use of force or threats, or make life difficult for you and the people closest to you. For these reasons, they are dangerous, even if they aren't criminal or violent because they can target the way people view you, your reputation, and any work or business-related arrangements you may have. If you find yourself in the aftermath of a breakup or distancing yourself from a malignant person, the "no contact" rule is your best option.

## 20. Employing the "No Contact" Rule

Once you leave a toxic, controlling situation or relationship, your best option is to stop any and all forms of contact with a person, and anyone they associate with. This becomes necessary to prevent further damage, or stop it completely. They can attempt to cause grief in your life, but if you take a stand and avoid interacting with them and taking their "bait", they will have fewer chances to connect with you. The No Contact Rule means:

- Deleting, blocking and stopping any and all contact on social media, online forums, and email

- Stop texting, calling, even to leave a message with your final thoughts and feelings. Simply stop and block all contact numbers

- Avoid where they work, live, and places they frequent, even if you don't contact them directly.

- If possible, avoid their family and friends, and anyone who may take their side

- If you find yourself running into them, you may ignore them, and if they persist in talking to you, make it clear that you no longer wish to contact them, and further incidents will be considered harassment. If it occurs again, contact the police and document any further incidents and attempts to contact you.

- Some people will convince a friend of theirs or yours to speak with you on their behalf, appealing to you as if they still care and want you to return. If this happens, make it clear to the friend or third-party contact that you are no longer in communication with the other person, and will accept no indirect or direct messages from them.

If you must maintain contact because of child custody or other another arrangement, consider a neutral third party who can make contact on your behalf, or have them present at all meetings. Stay firm and absolute in your decision to cut off contact. It can be difficult to manage when you still have an emotional connection. When you are facing this challenge, make sure to take time for yourself.

# Chapter 8: NLP and How it is Used to Convince and Persuade People

## 21. Analysis of Body Language and Communication: Non-Verbal

What is NLP and how is it used to persuade and manipulate people? When we consider methods of persuasion, we might consider the impact of words and dialogue that appeals to other people in order to lure them into following certain actions and behaviors. NLP is the acronym for neuro-linguistic programming, and it is a method developed to influence other people through non-verbal cues on the subconscious mind. This technique has been taught as a means to help people get want they want by using certain techniques that have an effect on the way others think, rendering them easier to listen and adhere to certain rules and practices. There is some controversy associated with NLP, including its varied effects on people and how much of an impact it has on others.

How is NLP used and who uses these methods? Salespeople, politicians and self-help gurus are often known for using techniques to persuade and read other people and using non-verbal methods of communication to impact how they influence others. While there are debates about NLP's effectiveness, a person who is highly skilled in this practice can read simple flinches, blushing or slight signs of discomfort to gauge their next move. They can detect these ones on one and in groups of people. Based on people's reactions, they might be able to determine what part of the brain is activated. For example, if a person responds favorably, they might be triggering endorphin release in the brain, which is a reward system. They may realize that making a specific gesture or speaking in certain tones can enhance this experience in others, therefore rendering them more susceptible to influence.

What else can people skilled in NLP determine from watching others? While the specific methods of NLP training are considered a form of pseudoscience and often debated, either because of its negative impact on people or whether it should be used in any form, are largely unknown to most people. Many self-help and impressionable personalities are trained in these methods and employ them often when addressing crowds at events or working with people one on one.

- They can determine what senses you are most likely to use or favor. They will pay close attention to your responses to observe whether your sense of hearing is strong and effective, picking up on details and asking questions based on what you hear, or whether you are more reactive to visuals or touch and/or scent. Knowing which of these senses you use the most can give them the advantage of employing techniques to draw you in and exploiting that sensitive part of your sensory system

- They will observe mannerisms, speech and movement patterns, including slight gestures. Over time, or even within a short span of time, they will begin to mimic your gestures and habits. This will not be as obvious as you might expect, and may cause you to feel connected and drawn to them; hence their method is working. We tend to trust and feel at ease with people who act and behave similarly to us because they are seen as less intimidating. Once we become comfortable with someone, we tend to let our guard down and become an easier target for manipulation and control

- Once an NLP expert knows which senses you favor most, they may incorporate them into their communication with you. For example, if they notice that you respond readily to visuals, they may validate what you say with "I see what you mean" or "I have the same view as you". Not only do these statements involve the words "see" and "view" in reference to visuals, but they also attempt to reassure an agreement between you and them, making you feel important and respected. Another example of using verbiage that corresponds to sensory preferences include "I feel what you mean", "I hear you" and "I'm touched by your comments".

- Once you let your guard down, the manipulation begins to take form, where your guard is down and you feel connected emotionally to the other person. During this stage, they are able to take more of a lead in conversations, using the mimicking of gestures and cues to "lead" you into doing what they want. They may not request or make demands outright, but rather, they will push their agenda gradually and in a

calculated manner so that by the time you are
under their control, you no longer realize it

- A skilled manipulator will use NLP to control
  you and all this time, you will believe that you
  are acting on your own without undue influence.
  You might view the person or source of
  influence as an inspiration or tool of life
  improvement, instead of seeing them as a
  means of control.

How can you guard yourself and others against the
dangers of NLP? The key is to notice early signs of this
practice to avoid becoming susceptible to the
influence of this dangerous method. The danger lies in
the nature of how NLP is applied, though a subtle
stream of insidious techniques that target the
subconscious.

- Look for signs that your body language, posture
  and language is being copied. Does the person
  sit in the same pose as you? If you change your
  posture or pose, do they follow suit? Chances
  are, they may notice your keen observation, and
  minimize they're mimicking to assure you that
  they are not practicing NLP.

- Try making a random gesture or movement to make yourself appear unpredictable, whether it's a slight shifting of your eyes or flicking your finger, wrist or another gesture they may not anticipate. You may notice a mirror image copying of some of your poses and gestures, which is the best time to switch up your own movements. This is important, because someone using NLP methods will observe eye movements to calculate what you're thinking, and they will look for specific patterns and trends. When you make a sudden change or shift in movement, it throws them off track and can complicate their attempt to control you

- Avoid letting anyone touch you if it is suspected they may be using NLP tactics. In fact, unless someone knows you well and you feel comfortable with them, like a close family or friend, avoid physical contact. During your interaction with them, you may become emotional, either happy, angry or sad. When this happens, they may reach out to touch you, even if briefly for a second, brushing your arm or offering an embrace. This is how they mark or anchor their touch to your emotional response. The effect it has is as follows: when they want to evoke a similar response in you, they will touch you in the same way, which can trigger your emotions similarly to when they initially patted your arm or gave you a hug. At all costs, avoid physical touch. If anyone attempts this, stand back and be firm. State that under no circumstance are they to touch you again.

- Be wary of vague language. This is used because in doing so, the speaker is able to avoid disagreements with you. They might act agreeable or accepting, without really establishing any reasons why. In conversing this way, they leave less room for challenge, controversy or division, and may induce a state of hypnosis, where you can become susceptible to persuasion without putting up a fight. To combat this method, use a specific language. When they refer to "opening your mind to invite ideas into your thought", ask: "what specific ideas and thought? How do these benefit my life?" Depending on the theme and direction of the conversation, specify further: are they referring to financial stability, self-discipline and/or mental health? If they avoid getting specific, back out of the conversation and avoid further contact with them.

- Take precautions when they use permissive or agreeable language and suggestions. This may include invitations to do what you like, to engage; however you feel comfortable, or phrases like "make yourself comfortable", "go ahead and say whatever you feel or like". In making these statements, you may feel as though there's no restriction or control they have over you, and these statements are used for this very reason: to fool your perception into feeling they are permissive and open-minded to everything so that you reveal more about yourself. As you open and reveal more about your thoughts, opinions, even your past mistakes and experiences, you're feeding the manipulator with many ideas they will use against you. At this point, it becomes almost effortless for them. If they are someone you socialize with, even enjoying a few drinks now and then, be careful not to let your guard down by consuming too much alcohol and getting attached to the person. They may seem benign and fun-loving as you are, only to become malignant when they find a vulnerability to exploit

- Sometimes, self-help aids and speakers use wording that sounds mysterious and almost nonsensical. For some people, they may interpret this as having profound meaning or sustenance, though if they were asked exactly what is meant, that likely wouldn't have a clue. Consider statements like "get in tune with your energy within to follow your natural path to success" as an example of something that seems profound, yet holds no true meaning. If anyone is prompted to expand or explicitly explain what they mean. They may ask you to go with your own flow or instincts when what they really mean is to become entranced in their own version of "freedom", which essentially means rendering full control to them

- People using NLP will add hidden words or meanings, often using innuendos. If confronted with doing so, they might deny it or act as if you misinterpreted them. If you don't pick up on these cues, they may have an effect on you later. For example, they may use double talk that hints towards a sexual advance, then retract what they've said later as if it was a joke or never said at all. They might repeat certain words or phrases, almost trance-like, to induce a similar effect on you. Be cautious about repetition and other methods that cause you to internalize and repeat those same words in your mind. This is how they imbed their ideas in you, causing you to feel and think in ways that make you more malleable to their tactics

- Always remain focused and alert around anyone exhibiting signs of NLP. This includes avoiding them when you feel tired or not at your best. You might think you are capable of handling certain people, and while you may be, there is a danger in underestimating the power of NLP and its effect on people. This can cause a lot of grief and heartache later when you realize how they've impacted your life.

- Always trust your instincts, even if you don't want to. Sometimes we ignore important signals that can detect harm because we are overwhelmed by influence from the person or people using these methods. It's much easier and less of an issue to simply enjoy their flattery and take it in. If we rarely experience this level of kindness, we might be tempted to go along with it, not understanding that it's completely fake and once we learn this, it can be hurtful. For these reasons, always keep vigilant and don't let anyone impact your emotions.

Always stay on guard around anyone who displays one or more of the above traits. Make a point of creating an NLP-proof layer that you can use as your defense. They will try to convince you that you're safe with them, and make you feel comfortable. Anyone going to great lengths to ensure your comfort, and continually convincing you to feel this way, is going to look for ways to break you down enough to get something from you. When in doubt, always figure out when you need to do for your own happiness, life and goals while accomplishing them. Don't let anyone convince you that you must follow a specific path or set of ideas. This will only lead to deception and manipulation. Keeping yourself involved with your own life and goals is most helpful and a better way to life.

### 22. How to Use These Skills to Understand the People in Our Lives and Those We Meet for the First Time

It's important to understand our own needs and rights, reminding ourselves often, so that when we come into contact with a toxic person, we can handle them effectively. It's especially important to pay attention to people we meet for the first time and determine how they impact us initially and later on in life. Keep in mind the following as you find someone new, either in a relationship or friendship, and/or become faced with an invitation to join a group or organization:

- What are your benefits versus theirs? If someone proposes an idea or concept right away, it almost always has a benefit for them. They may try to convince you there is something in it for you as well, though be cautious and avoid falling for anything too good to be true. Chances are, if they have to use effort to convince you, you're not going to benefit, and may find yourself in a worse position later

- Are they quick to flatter and give you compliments? Aside from a natural, pleasant nature or compliment, which isn't odd or unusual, beware of anyone trying too hard to impress you or make you feel "high" or euphoric. This will eventually run its course and take a turn for the worse behavior.

- When you express your ideas or thoughts, do they understand and listen to fir interest or simply to say or do something in return? Look for signs they may try to gain your trust too soon.

It is possible to use some aspects of NLP skills, even in a general sense, to learn about other people and how they interact with us. Always look for patterns in behavior that are persuasive and malignant in nature. If you don't trust them, or if they seem difficult to understand, this can be a sign that they are not who they seem. Imagine if you were to use NLP or similar techniques on them to test their effectiveness? If you are uncertain about their true plans, take a moment to consider the following:

- If you mirror their body language, eye movements, and gestures, would they notice? Would they be less aware if you did this gradually over time?

- Are you going to receive the same response from them, whether you use specific or vague language? If so, how will this impact how you communicate with them?

- How would they respond to compliments and similar statements from you? Would they enjoy the attention or regard you with suspicion?

- Watch for gestures or signs of avoidance when you confront them about what they say or do. They may abandon you completely if you're too much "work" to manipulate.

Remember, a manipulator will always begin by telling you something you want to hear. You may want to believe them wholeheartedly. They want you to have complete trust in them, without any reservations and are sometimes willing to spend a lot of time and effort to convince you to place your confidence in them completely. Once you recognize these tactics, you'll be

better prepared to handle situations where you
suspect early signs of mind control and manipulation.

# Chapter 9: Dark Psychology

### 23. What is Dark Psychology?

Dark psychology is the study of how certain people prey upon others for the sole purpose of control, manipulation, and victimization. People who are capable of cold and calculated manipulative techniques without any remorse or concern for the other person are often sociopathic, one of the three personality types in the dark triad model, along with narcissism and Machiavellianism. There are certain traits and attributes that people share, in addition to possessing all or most of the three personalities on the dark triad:

- There is a general lack of remorse and no concern about the impact of their actions on others

- They are indifferent to the suffering and ill effects of their actions on others, as long as their goal is achieved.

- A narcissist or sociopath may pretend to have your best interests in mind, yet they become eagerly persuasive too quickly and too soon.

- They are not interested in you as a person, though they will learn as much as they can to use against you when it suits them.

Mind control is the ultimate goal by manipulative people who resemble the character of the dark triad. Anyone who uses persuasion, manipulation and coercion in one way or another is employing dark triad techniques, and sometimes this can be done when there is no harm intended. Reverse psychology is one example of how saying the opposite of what you want the other person expects can convince them to change what they are doing. This is often used by parents with children, where instead of telling the kids to be quiet, they ask them to shout and yell loudly. When this happens, the trigger response is to do the exact opposite, by switching what their original intentions are. The child(ren) may suddenly become quiet, taking the opposite approach.

A skilled manipulator will convince you that the decisions they influence you to make are of your own free will. This can be especially harmful when you no longer know whether you control your own thoughts. Dark psychological methods can become ingrained in thought patterns, repeating phrases, and ideas stated by the manipulator, which can be employed through various techniques, including NLP, which is covered in chapter 8.

### 24. How Dark Psychology Exploits to Keep Us Down and Achieving Complete Control

Knowing how dark psychology works is about taking a look at what makes us a target for a narcissist or sociopath. We may think of ourselves as intelligent, confident and generally fool-proof, though manipulation is not always specific. Some victims of dark psychology methods of control and manipulation are completely unaware, or sometimes dismiss and suspicions they may have about someone who exhibits controlling methods.

# Chapter 10: Who Uses Dark Psychology?

The people who employ dark psychology methods:
politicians, religious leaders, cults, lawyers,
narcissists, other people in a powerful and influential
position

A wide variety of people use mind control methods.
This is a fact that can often be dismissed because
most of us think of a manipulator in a certain way, or
as a certain type of person. We might automatically
picture someone powerful or craving power, or a very
influential, popular person who effortlessly convinces
people to follow and revere them, much like a cult
leader or a celebrity. Politicians, religious leaders, cult
leaders, lawyers, and other people with narcissistic
traits often fit within the dark triad definition. Within
our own social and familial circles, we can also find
many instances of dark psychological methods used to
keep us within certain parameters, and under
someone's control. They can cause a massive change
in a

Politicians have a strong impact on the public,
especially when they are on center stage during a
campaign or making headlines in the news regularly.

Whether they are respected, despised, or seen as unimportant, they continue to influence everyone around them and the masses around their country and the world, who are constantly watching the news.

## 25. Becoming Aware of Dark Psychology Tactics and Guarding Yourself Against Them

The following are examples of dark psychology methods used in everyday situations:

**Example 1**

Shane is invited to a rally by his friend Gary who read about a groundbreaking political platform from a new candidate. The candidate is young and raised in a family that owns several development businesses and other ventures. The candidate is inexperienced in politics, but he's savvy and knows a lot of people in Shane and Gary's community, including business owners and local celebrities. He prides himself on this popularity and promises something beneficial to everyone, without any specifics. When Shane notices a lack of direction and possible negative effects on his city, he lets Gary know, who dismisses Shane's concerns, because Gary feels excited to join a campaign team to work closely with the candidate.

Shane notices that his best friend has withdrawn from communicating, and barely hears from him anymore. When he tries to approach Gary at a local store, he finds that his friend is a very different person. Gary's wife and family eventually notice these changes and notice a great deal of his time was sacrificed to work on the campaign. It isn't until after the election, when another candidate wins, that Shane begins to see his friend more often, and no longer until the spell of the young, manipulative politician.

**Example 2**

Sasha is a fan of self-improvement and believes in the power of hypnosis, which helped him overcome smoking and other habits. When he learns of a self-help seminar, he's eager to register and take part in the event. His friend Jean warms him that it could be expensive and may not be as beneficial nor practical in life. Jean urges Sasha to research the speaker and find out why they have such a cult following and has become wealthy because of his speeches. Sasha dismisses the idea and is excited to attend, so he readily signs up instead. At the event, he becomes mesmerized by the stage presence and quickly joins in the mantras and chants shared with the audience.

During intermission, he has a chance to meet the speaker, becoming further impressed by the methods mentioned on stage. He buys a book and some information from the booth selling self-help books, and leaves feeling "high". Sometime later, he becomes bored with the book, not even finishing it, and experiences difficulty understanding what some of the vague concepts and ideas are. After some reflection, he realizes the whole set up was a gimmick and a means to get people thrilled about positive changes in life, without any real, tangible solutions. The self-help guru achieved high sales of his books, merchandise and speech tickets without providing any real benefit to anyone, expect the illusion of happiness and success.

Considering both examples, it's easy to become influenced by someone we regard as an expert or confident in a specific field, whether it's politics, business or making improvements in life. Initially, it doesn't feel like manipulation, and when the person or concept is already popular on television or social media, it's easier to accept and embrace. There is a lot of branding and marketing that creates a buzz in public, both in real life and online. By saturating your virtual world and reality, there is little preventing you from seeing promotional material, when ads and banners are everywhere. Virtual boundaries are difficult to maintain because we are subject to anything the market decides to post at any time.

# Chapter 11: Leaving Behind the Chains of Mind Control and Living a Happy, Free Life

## 26. How to Break Free from the Constraints and Emotions that Others have Programmed and Led us to Accept

Breaking free from mind control is not an easy task, though it is possible with a clear determination and plan. Understanding who we are, what we truly want and our goals are important in establishing and maintaining a clear path in life. This is one of the key ways to stay on track with your goals, along with the following:

- Set your own rules. It's your life to live, and you have the right to establish boundaries and guidelines by how you wish to live.

- Make your own goals, and if you want to change them, it's your right to do so. While it's important to finish what you start, there are some circumstances where it can become impossible or unfeasible. Be realistic and adjust your milestones and achievements to what suits you.

- You don't owe anyone an explanation about your life or decisions. Make your own choices on your terms, and don't change because you're pressured. No one can determine what's best for you but yourself.

In some societies and cultures, we might feel compelled to adhere to certain ideals, with the expectations of achieving traditional or academic roles. This is also a factor in relationships, where roles are defined with little or no room for change. When this is strictly followed, it can lead to situations where people are vulnerable to manipulation, as their actions and goals are predictable and contained in a community. These factors can make altering your plans difficult, though people take on challenges and change the course for others as well. This is a positive way to become a leader, by influencing others through your own actions and achievements, instead of using manipulation to control them.

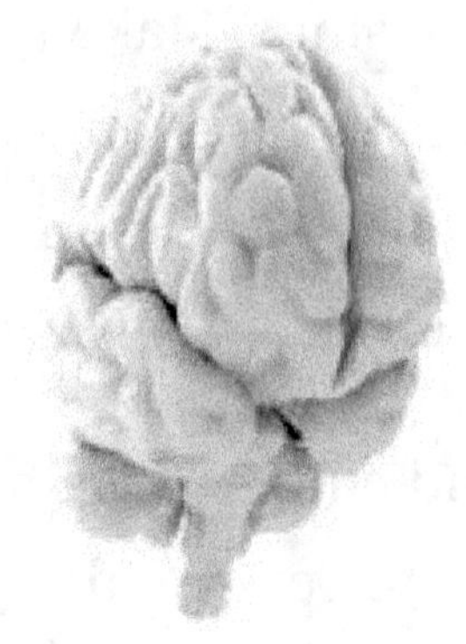

# Chapter 12: The Importance of Thought Patterns

### 27. How Do You Talk to Yourself? What is Your Internal Dialogue?

How we view and talk to ourselves has a profound effect on us and the way we live. Our internal dialogue is a reflection of what others have said and continue to say to us over time. If we often hear criticism or perceive what others say to be critical of us, then we will internalize and regurgitate the same or similar information, causing us to believe that we are not worthy or good enough. Positive reinforcement and constructive input, on the other hand, can provide a strong foundation for positive thoughts and confidence building. Consider some of the following expressions or comments you might communicate internally:

"You don't have the capability to do this."

"There is always someone better than you for the job. Why would they pick you?"

"Are you sure this wants you to want? Are you really meant for this?"

The above phrases are full of self-doubt and questioning, causing you to second-guess your ability to accomplish and/or achieve a goal. While you may be hearing these statements as a voice in your head, or a persistent thought, consider its source: a current or previous, pervasive dialogue from someone making you feel inadequate and unable to perform a task or incapable in general. You might have heard something negative from a current or previous employer, or as a child, constant comparison to others and emotionally neglected as a result. When we feel as though there is no positive reinforcement in our lives, we might blame ourselves, then internalize the negative, which sets an ugly foundation that doesn't serve to help us at all.

Resetting the internal dialogue is a powerful way to regain the power you have in life and establish a positive foundation. Consider that while you may have had negative treatment at some point in your life, you don't have to replay those messages in your mind on repeat, and you deserve to have the same opportunities and positive reinforcement as anyone else. Changing this pattern consists of making a shift into affirmations, which help remind us of our value

and give us internal strength to build something
positive and worthwhile.

## 28. How Do Others Talk to you? And you Believe Them?

The way people treat us impacts our view of ourselves
and how we allow them to continue treating (or
mistreating) us. Often, we are not aware of the impact

of others' statements, because we might think we ignore them and move on, without much thought. Subconsciously, we will retain some of the negativity, which will have an impact on how we view ourselves, without our knowing it completely. We may not realize how the seemingly insignificant jabs of a coworker or bullying of a relative might contribute to feelings of inadequacy and self-doubt.

# Chapter 13: From Freedom of Thought to Unconditional Happiness

## 29. Having the Courage to Think Freely and Feel Entitled to Choose How to Live on Your Own Terms and Generate Unconditional Happiness

Breaking free from negative thinking and feelings is a process that takes time and effort to achieve. We may not realize how important this is until we are faced with a situation that challenges our own self-view, such as a job interview where the employer or human resources manager asks us to describe who we are and what our strengths are. At that very moment, are we aware of what we are good at and if so, do we honestly believe in ourselves or simply state what they want to hear? Are we more apt to think of our flaws and mistakes than our achievements in life?

Daily affirmations are excellent in establishing a new set of rules or thoughts that we internalize about ourselves. These allow us to acknowledge that while we may not be perfect, we have value and good attributes that count for more than we may realize. These affirmations also help set a pattern of "I can do this" in your mind, to counteract the negative that has been instilled for too long. We often don't realize how impactful the criticism is until we make a change towards the positive. Consider the following examples of affirmations that can start your new life for an improved outlook on life:

"I'm in control of my life, and I can choose what foundation I build and how it will support my choices."

This is a powerful way of taking a strong stance away from dependency and establishing that you alone are responsible for your own happiness and satisfaction in life. Only you can set the tone and strength or your achievements, and avoid the negativity from other people and situations. Choose to build something solid and well-suited to your needs, so that it becomes an anchor in a sea of criticism and self-doubt.

"I am above the negativity in my head. I am better than them, and I will conquer them."

This is a strong phrase that can be used internally as a defense against negativity when it sneaks its way into your thoughts and ideas. This may cause you to realize how often negative and self-defeating comments are within us, making us feel less worthy or ideal as a result. Recognizing that these are occurring is one major step in eradicating negativity while reinforcing a better way of thinking through empowering statements like this one will help tear down the critiques and replace them with motivation.

"I have my health and my mind. Both of these are strong and will help me achieve anything."

Often, we might take for granted our inner strengths, whether we have good health, or are able to function and achieve in spite of challenges (health-related and other obstacles). We might discount our abilities when others are consistently critical or negative towards us, which doesn't help our case. We might also ignore valuable traits we already have, like perseverance and resilience when we are against competitors. We may not realize the challenges other people face, many of them unable to accomplish what we can because of various circumstances. For this reason, we can express the gratitude that we have a good foundation for building a better life and goals to achieve.

"I have what it takes to be successful."

We all need to remind ourselves of this now and again, to reinforce the idea that we are capable of greatness, and have the tools to get ourselves there. Success is measured in how we handle situations, including failure, as an error is a stepping stone to learn from and move on from. Sometimes, we cannot progress until we make our own mistakes and learn from them. This is powerful in helping us learn authentically, and first-hand, through our own sense of trial-and-error, and while it is not easy to develop our goals this way, it can build a much stronger base in the long-term. Success is a mindset, and only you have the right to decide what it means to you. You do not have to live according to another person's view or ideal on success.

"I have the courage to stand up for myself and can speak my mind."

You deserve to be heard and feel strong inside. No one should be able to take it from you, though it can happen, and it can feel devastating when we are hurt or put down. When this happens, and depending on the individual circumstances and situation, we have the ability to stand up and make a statement or simply walk away from negativity. Standing up for yourself doesn't have to be confrontational or ignite a debate. This can simply involve saying something like, "I'm not going to listen to any more of your criticism" or "I've had enough of these negative comments. I'm not going to listen to them anymore." If you need time to develop the courage to speak these aloud, practice on your own until you feel comfortable in doing so.

"I will abandon bad habits and establish new, more positive ones."

Discard the bad thoughts, and recurring negativity stuck in your head. This will only weigh you down and make you feel less worthy of better options in life. Simply stating this affirmation to yourself every morning has a cleansing effect. It is mental preparation for cleaning away and existing or residual bad thoughts, replacing them with thoughts of "I can do this". Focus every day on the tasks and goals you are set to achieve and make it a priority to re-state, "I can do____" each day. This will give you the internal motivation you need to succeed and make a better start to your day, every day.

"The difficult times are temporary, and they will pass."

When we experience difficult situations, including traumatic or life-changing events, it can seem impossible to move ahead or focus on anything but what we are going through. We often have to recognize this as a reality we face, thought despite it, we can remind ourselves that life continues to wait for us, and is ready once we decide to move ahead and continue living once again. Sometimes taking a pause or a break is a good idea, though making the most out of this time should include proper self-care and regular affirmations to maintain and build self-confidence. Once you realize the power of your mind and how you can positively influence your way of thinking, you'll notice a major shift in life for yourself and those who rely on you.

## 30. What Exactly is Unconditional Happiness?

You deserve to be happy, regardless of the outcome of one scenario or another, whether you achieve a measure of greatness or not. To experience true happiness, we have to step away from our challenges in life, even the positive, just to reaffirm that we have a right to be happy. To find and harvest unconditional happiness means we embrace our life at the moment, without any conditions, and choose to be grateful for everything we already have. All too often, we might consider how much better off we would be with a better job, more money and other situations that we might want to change. When this occurs, we might not realize how these goals, while admirable and worth pursuing, should never stand as a way to put off our happiness.

When considering the meaning of unconditional love, we might think of a parent who loves their children, regardless of who they are and how they choose to love their life. We often read studies and information on how parental support and love can and will greatly improve the quality of children's lives, increasing their chances of success, and making a better life for themselves. In a similar way, we have to give ourselves this same level of full, unconditional love, which contributes to unconditional happiness and improves our life greatly.

One of the greatest drawbacks in life for many people is striving for conditional happiness, specifically in Western culture, where we focus on material gain and high paying jobs, among similar goals as a measure of true success that will make us happy. We may actually put off or postpone our own sense of happiness and joy because we don't like where we are now in life, even if our position is stable, and we are in a good position to move ahead. Chasing after goals and dreams is admirable, though it should never be accompanied by "I won't be satisfied or happy until I reach this goal" or "I can't be happy until I ____". These conditional versions of happiness will only serve as a disappointment when you realize that problems and challenges will continually be a part of life, even where we may not see them in our future. Our goal should be happiness first, then building and achieving our goals, and always working to weather any challenges or changes that we encounter along the way.

### 31. Freeing Yourself From Anxiety, Stress, Depression, and Other Factors that Keep us Down

Society is ever-changing and new technology and innovation of today seem to be in the distant past tomorrow, as we live in an ever-increasing fast-paced world with many opportunities and challenges at once. In order to make the best of it, we may become ambitious, looking for any and all chances to strive for goals, only to find more challenges over time. For many people, life is also riddled with a lot of responsibility and constraints, much of which we can struggle with on a regular basis. This can lead to exhaustion and stress, and in time, may lead to depression, anxiety and other disorders that impact many people around the world from all backgrounds and lifestyles. From fast-paced business people to those of us who are more laid-back and take a different approach to life, the reality of anxiety, stress, and depression are real and can impact anyone. When this happens, we need to take an inventory of our lives and determine where the stressors are, in order to minimize them as much as possible. This isn't an easy process and can result in some difficult decisions along the way.

## 32. How to Live a Free and Positive Life

How you choose to live your life is ultimately your decision. We may be impacted by what others say, how they react and interact with us, though, in the end, we are responsible for our own happiness. As we learn to accept life as it unfolds for us, we realize that happiness and becoming content doesn't hinge on our success or how perfect we appear to other people, but rather, it stems from the internal gratification we feel inside for our life and how we appreciate the people and positivity in our life.

# Chapter 14: Conclusion

### 33. The 7 Habits of Dark Psychology: What are They?

In reviewing the signs and characteristics of dark psychology, there are seven traits or habits that we can look for in order to guard ourselves against the pitfalls of this malignant personality. A summary of each habit can be described as follows:

### *1. The Manipulation*

The use of pervasive techniques to instill fear, bullying tactics and other forms of control to force someone to act and/or behave in a certain way are all characteristics of manipulation.

### *2. The Persuasion*

Persuasion, a lesser evil in comparison to manipulation, can still be used with ill intentions, where the person being persuaded has little or nothing to gain as a result. Some forms of persuasion can be difficult to detect initially, which makes it a challenge to notice, though manipulation will follow

### 3. Exploit Vulnerabilities

Weaknesses are what they look for and use against you. A manipulator will listen intently to learn what you fear the most and take advantage of you when it suits their plan.

### 5.  The Brainwashing

A manipulator will use techniques, often subtle at first, to watch for weaknesses and vulnerabilities, so they can target you to believe everything they say and do. They will use subtle gestures and non-verbal communication to control and gain your trust.

### 6. The Body Reading

Your non-verbal cues are what manipulators read and keep an eye on, to learn about your weaknesses. They use techniques used in NLP (neuro-linguistic programming)

### 3. Offer Demotivating Words to Propose Themselves as a Solution

Never take anything a manipulative person takes to heart. Keep in mind they have no good intentions for you, and anything expressed, whether it's positive or negative, serves their purpose only.

### *7. Put the Chains to Your Thoughts and Your Emotions*

The dark triad or personalities will enslave your emotions and thoughts as much as possible, to gain control over every aspect of your life.

In conclusion, it's important to keep the following seven points of the dark triad in mind at all times, to gauge the possibility of mind control techniques. In most cases, you'll find that people are well-intentioned and good in their ideas and thoughts, while the few who try to influence and manipulate you will eventually deviate from their mask of kindness, and reveal who they really are. When this happens, you'll be well prepared to make an informed decision.